ADVENTUROUS
ARMADA

Miguel Lopez de Legazpi

From painting in Museo-Biblioteca de Ultramar, Madrid

Adventurous

Armada

THE STORY OF LEGAZPI'S EXPEDITION

ANDREW SHARP

Whitcombe & Tombs Ltd

First published by
Whitcombe and Tombs Ltd
Christchurch, New Zealand
1961

PRINTED AND PUBLISHED BY
WHITCOMBE AND TOMBS LTD
CHRISTCHURCH AUCKLAND WELLINGTON DUNEDIN
HAMILTON LOWER HUTT TIMARU INVERCARGILL
LONDON MELBOURNE SYDNEY PERTH GEELONG

Contents

ILLUSTRATIONS

I

Gentlemen Adventurers
& Others

IN the middle months of the year 1561, all was hustle and bustle in the little port of La Navidad, on the west coast of Mexico. Here, by order of King Philip of Spain, preparations for an expedition across the North Pacific to the Isles of the West were being made, and news had just arrived that Miguel Lopez de Legazpi, a wealthy Spanish gentleman of Mexico City, had been appointed to the command. The ships for the expedition had already been building for three years. Yet it was to be three years more before the Armada sailed at the end of 1564. There were two large galleons, and two smaller ships. They were made of local timber, and many logs, including curved ones for the ribs, had to be selected, sawn, transported to the stocks, and adzed to shape for the keels, frames and masts. Planks were sawn for the decks and sides. After the hulls were launched, the super-structures, high in the poop and forecastle in the fashion of the time, with a lower waist, were built up. Ships' boats were made, as well as furniture.

While this was going on at La Navidad, the rigging and cables were being made at ports on the west coast of Guate-mala, to the south of Mexico, where a hemp substitute made from a local plant called *pita* was used. The cordage was then taken by ship up the coast to La Navidad, something like thirty tons of this rope being required.

Another need that was provided locally was ship's biscuit, which was the main item in hard rations for a prospective period of two years. The grain was grown specially, and problems of harvesting, making the biscuit, and transporting it to the ships in the dry season to avoid mould were involved.

In addition to these local materials, there were a hundred and one items which had to be brought from Spain. Many of them were relatively easy to transport across Mexico to La Navidad by carts, the main difficulty being the fording of two rivers. The biggest job, however, was to get the heavy anchors, guns and cannon-balls to their destination. This involved handling from Vera Cruz on the east coast of Mexico southwards to the mouth of the River Coatzacoalcas by ship, a dangerous voyage of two or three days in cross-winds from the sea; then by river-boats up the river some 150 miles to a landing-place; then 60 miles overland by carts to Tehuantepec on the west coast; and then by ship again 750 miles along the west coast to La Navidad.

La Navidad was an isolated and unhealthy port, and it was therefore hard to get carpenters, smiths and other skilled craftsmen to go there. The rate of sickness and death was high.

Among the most important people to the expedition were the pilots, who were in charge both of the navigation and the working of the ships. Some of them were in La Navidad for some time before the expedition was due to sail. The two smaller vessels were completed and put into service before the larger ones were finished, fetching and carrying up and down the coast. One of these smaller vessels was named the *San Juan*, the other the *San Lucas*.

Before this story is finished, it will be agreed that the name of the *San Lucas* deserves to be one of the most renowned in the annals of the sea, like that of its pilot Lope Martin, although the word notorious would perhaps be more appropriate for the pilot himself.

Lope Martin's home, so far as an itinerant pilot had a home, was in Ayamonte, a small sea-port on the south-west coast of Spain. It was on sea-ports such as Ayamonte that Spanish sea-power and empire were built. At Huelva, just along the coast from Ayamonte, Columbus had concerted with the Pinzons and other seafarers in preparing that expedition which found a new world in the Americas. Lope Martin was of Portuguese descent. This again is not surprising, since Ayamonte is not far from the Portuguese border, and the Portuguese sea-going tradition was then in its prime.

Slowly but surely the difficulties of finishing the two big ships at La Navidad were overcome. In June 1564 the two smaller vessels, the *San Juan* and the *San Lucas*, brought the masts and spars to the galleons, and the work of rigging them proceeded rapidly.

In the later stages of the preparation of the ships at La Navidad, a conspiracy developed among some pilots and sailors of dubious allegiance to the Spanish cause. Of these there were plenty, for the rapid expansion of Spain's overseas empire had meant that the crews of her ships included many Portuguese, Italian, French and Greek sailors.

The instigator of the plot was a French pilot, Pierres Plun. Plun's plan was that the conspirators should steal the *San Lucas*, go to the East Indies and get a load of gold and spices, and then sail with it to France. Prominent among the plotters were Lope Martin, the pilot of the *San Lucas*, and his crony Juan Jañiz, a Portuguese sailor on the *San Lucas*. The *San Lucas*, being small and fast, was well suited to the plan, since not many sailors were needed to work it, and it could show a clean pair of heels to the other ships. Plun persuaded another pilot named Jaymes Fortun, a Venetian, to throw in

his lot with them. Fortun's cousin, Juan Maria, a master and
ship's gunner, and a ship's mate named Jorge the Greek,
were other ringleaders. A number of sailors were enticed
into the scheme by the prospect of loot. The conspirators
waited for an opportunity to make off with the *San Lucas*.

Meanwhile in Mexico City the gilt on Legazpi's ginger-
bread was wearing thin. When he accepted the command of
the expedition in 1561, he and everybody else thought that
the Armada would be away within a year. Legazpi, with
typical and indeed unavoidable generosity, kept open house
for the officers and gentlemen, and supported large numbers
of soldiers, even supplying them with arms and equipment
at his own expense. But when the time of waiting for the
completion at La Navidad of the building of the ships grew
from one year to two, and then to a third, even Legazpi's
resources began to wilt.

What does a gentleman adventurer who has accepted the
command of a royal expedition do when he finds himself
financially embarrassed as a result? Legazpi sold his *hacienda*
in Mechoacan to a relative of his friend and neighbour Lope
de Sosa for 40,000 pesos. By the time the expedition sailed,
he had expended some 100,000 pesos.

For the beginning of the chain of events which led Legazpi
to exchange the role of a wealthy private citizen of Mexico
City for that of a would-be *conquistador* we must go back to
1521. That was the year when Ferdinand Magellan, coming
across the Pacific after traversing the Strait of Magellan,
discovered first Guam in the Marianas, and then the southern
Philippines. In these latter islands Magellan flung away his
life in trying to demonstrate to the chief of Zebu the power
of European arms against the people of the nearby Mactan.
For once the spear prevailed over the arquebus, and the
Spaniards were forced to retreat from Mactan, leaving their
dead commander behind. But the Philippines were on the

map as a magnet to Spanish ships for three and a half centuries afterwards.

In 1526 the *Santa Maria de la Victoria* followed in Magellan's wake round South America to Guam and the East Indies. One of the senior officers was Andres de Urdaneta. On this first visit by Urdaneta to the Indies, he remained until 1535, when he returned to Spain round South Africa in Portuguese ships.

Meanwhile Cortes, the conqueror of Mexico, was pacifying that country as a bright jewel added to the Spanish Crown. Mexico City became the Spanish capital, with Vera Cruz, on the east coast, as the port of access to New Spain from Cuba and Spain itself.

In or about 1530, Miguel Lopez de Legazpi had arrived in Mexico City as a young Spanish colonist of some 21 years of age. In 1538 his kinsman Andres de Urdaneta, the veteran of the *Santa Maria de la Victoria*, came to Mexico also. The Urdanetas and Legazpis were the descendants of ancient families of Guipuzcoa in Spain.

In 1542 a fleet of six ships under Ruy Lopez de Villalobos sailed from the west coast of Mexico for the Isles of the West. The Isles of the West – *Las Islas del Poniente* – was the Spanish name for the East Indies from the Philippines to New Guinea. All of Villalobos's six ships were lost in the East Indies, and eventually the survivors returned to Europe by the route round South Africa.

In 1553 Urdaneta, the veteran soldier and former circumnavigator of the world, took the habit of an Augustinian monk in Mexico. His kinsman Legazpi had by that time become one of the most prosperous and respected citizens of Mexico City.

One day in 1559 Don Luis de Velasco, the Spanish Viceroy in Mexico City, who had the responsibility of organizing a new expedition to the Isles of the West at the bidding of King Philip of Spain, gave Urdaneta a letter from the King himself.

'Devout Father Fray Andres de Urdaneta of the Order of Saint Augustine,' wrote King Philip, 'I have been told that when you were a layman you went . . . through the Strait of Magellan, and to the Spice Islands where you stayed eight years in our service. And since we have charged Don Luis de Velasco, Our Viceroy of New Spain, to send two ships for the discovery of the Isles of the West in the vicinity of the Moluccas, and to tell them what they must do, in accordance with the instruction I have sent him; and since, according to the great knowledge and understanding you are said to have of those parts, knowing well their navigation, and being a fine cosmographer, it would be of great advantage that you should go in those ships both for matters of navigation and for the service of our Lord God and Ourselves: I ask and charge you to go in the ships, and do what the Viceroy asks you, that in addition to the service you would do our Lord, I may be well served, and I bid you note these things so that you may receive a fitting reward.'

With this letter went another from the King to Urdaneta's ecclesiastical superior, the Provincial of the Augustinian Order in New Spain, asking him to free Urdaneta for the commission that had been devised for him.

With auspices so august, it is not surprising that Urdaneta wrote back to the King accepting the charge, while at the same time saying that he was a veteran whose health had been undermined by his adventurous life. At this time Urdaneta was well into his sixties.

Whereas the Viceroy had invoked the royal intervention in order to secure the services of Urdaneta for the expedition, the choice of other leaders was in the Viceroy's hands. Thus it was that early in 1561 Don Luis decided to ask Miguel Lopez de Legazpi, the well-born, wealthy and respected

citizen of Mexico City, to head the expedition. There is
some evidence that the Viceroy had been shopping around
for a suitable leader before approaching Legazpi, and that
others had declined the doubtful privilege of leading a new
expedition in the track of those of Magellan, Saavedra and
Villalobos, all of whom had lost their lives in the Isles of the
West.

At an interview the Viceroy told his good friend Legazpi
of what he had in mind for him. He explained that the King's
command was that the expedition should try to find a
foothold in the Isles of the West outside the possessions of
the King of Portugal, so that the gold and spices which were
thought to be present in all those islands might be sent
back to Mexico and Spain. For this it was essential that a
way be found of sailing back east to Mexico, for by agreement
the western parts of the Indies belonged to the King of
Portugal. Legazpi as leader must expect to have many
demands on his private purse, but if a way of sailing back to
Mexico direct were found, and Legazpi were successful in
making a settlement in the Isles of the West, the Viceroy
promised to ask the King of Spain to authorize the payment
to Legazpi of 4000 ducats, and to reward him with concessions
for trade and mining and pearl fisheries, as well as other
honours.

Legazpi accepted the command, thereby opening up the
way to his transformation from a well-to-do private citizen
into a *conquistador*.

It may seem strange that a man without experience in
navigation or war, without salary and at considerable expense
to himself, should have been the commander of a royal
expedition to foreign parts comprising several armed sailing
ships. This was, however, long before the days of organized
naval services. It was the Spanish custom to appoint men of
family as the captains of the King's ships, with professional

pilots to look after the navigation and the crews. Gentlemen adventurers like Magellan and Legazpi, going off in a few ships to the ends of the earth, in those days changed the history of the world.

It is abundantly clear from the opinions of his fellows, and from his acts themselves, that Miguel Lopez de Legazpi was an able and a good man, with a liberal attitude to the native peoples among whom he spent most of his life, an ability to lead men by encouragement rather than the iron fist, generous, and tempering justice with mercy.

Legazpi, who was at this time in his fifties, now consulted with the Viceroy concerning the filling of other posts. As a result several members of Legazpi's own circle in Mexico City were approached. Foremost among these was Legazpi's grandson, Felipe de Salcedo. Felipe accepted, and the sequel showed that he was made of the same mixture of energy and good sense as his grandfather.

Another of Legazpi's chosen leaders was Juan de la Isla, a man then in his forties, who had been a friend of the Legazpis in Mexico City for the best part of ten years. Isla joined the expedition as the captain of one of the ships, of which his brother Rodrigo was pilot.

It would seem, from the requests they later made to the King, that Legazpi and his friends and relatives in Mexico City were by no means blind to the opportunities for wealth and power that the successful accomplishment of the enterprise might bring.

In July 1564 Legazpi's friend the Viceroy of New Spain, Don Luis de Velasco, died. As a mark of Legazpi's status he was chosen to bear the Royal Standard at the Viceroy's funeral.

The final sending off of the expedition now fell to the Real Audiencia in Mexico City – a council of magistrates, headed for the time by the Visitor-General of New Spain, Valderrama.

One day soon after the Viceroy's death, Juan Pablo de Carrion appeared before Valderrama at his own request. As Almirante designate he would be second-in-command after Legazpi. Carrion was a survivor of Villalobos's expedition across the Pacific some twenty years previously. Like Urdaneta, therefore, he knew something of the East Indies and had voyaged round the world. Carrion complained that Andres de Urdaneta had had the ear of the late Viceroy to such effect that it had been ordered that they try first and foremost to find the east coast of New Guinea and make their settlement there. Carrion, however, thought that there were very good reasons why they should not. In 1544 the *San Juan* of the expedition of Villalobos had come east from the East Indies along the coast of New Guinea for 380 leagues, and in all that journey they were able to buy but little food from the negroes there. No one had probed those seas from the east, and to do so with their big ships would be full of danger. If on the other hand they went direct to the Philippines, argued Carrion, they could expect following winds, as Villalobos's Armada had found in 1542. The Philippines were known to be fertile, rich and large, and to the north of them was China. They were well placed for a direct return to New Spain if such were possible.

Valderrama considered these matters and decided in his own mind that there was good sense in what Carrion said. But there was Urdaneta to be reckoned with, and Urdaneta was obdurate – so obdurate, in fact, that he said he would not go if Carrion had his way. Furthermore Legazpi, being so close to Urdaneta, and having no direct experience of his own to go on, supported the Friar's opinion.

This was indeed a hot potato for Valderrama and the Real Audiencia to have to handle on the very eve of the departure

HAWAII

MEXICO

La Navidad
Acapulco

CLS

EQUATOR

PHOENIX
GROUP

JOKELAUS

MARQUESAS

SAMOA

TUAMOTUS

COOKS

TAHITI

TONGA

AUSTRALS

The Pacific Area

of the captains, gentlemen, monks and soldiers for the coast.
The Real Audiencia, in finalizing their instructions to
Legazpi, had to decide what to do on this knotty and vital
matter, which might well decide whether the nucleus of a
new Spanish empire would be in New Guinea or the
Philippines.

On 1 September, 1564, Valderrama and the learned
magistrates of the Real Audiencia, at a formal ceremony,
bestowed on Legazpi the document embodying their final
instructions. Legazpi was told not to open it until the Armada
was 100 leagues out from Mexico.

There were present at this ceremony the magistrates of
the Real Audiencia, Doctor Ceynos, Doctor Villalobos,
Doctor Orosco, Doctor Vasco de Puga and Doctor Villa-
nueva, as well as Valderrama. A graphic picture of the
occasion is summoned to the mind's eye by the record of
Antonio de Turcios, the Chief Scribe of the Government of
New Spain: 'In the City of Mexico on the first day of the
month of September of 1564, the Lords and Judges of the
Real Audiencia of New Spain, in the presence of me,
Antonio de Turcios, Chief Scribe of the Government, being
in accord, ordered the delivery of, and so delivered, this
Instruction affirmed by the said Lords and Judges, com-
prising 14 pages, to Miguel Lopez de Legazpi, Governor and
Captain-General of the Armada which, by order of His
Majesty, is being sent to the discovery of the Isles of the
West, so that he may implement the Instruction, and keep to
and comply with it in all the details contained therein.
The said Miguel Lopez de Legazpi took possession of the
said Instruction, and promised and swore by God our Lord
and by the Sign of the Cross on which he physically placed
his right hand, and by the words of the four Holy Evangels,
and made a solemn oath, as a Gentleman, his hands joined
with and placed between those of the Illustrious Señor

Licenciado Valderrama of the Council of His Majesty and his Visitor-General of New Spain, Chevalier, Gentleman, once, twice and thrice, once, twice and thrice, once, twice and thrice, to go in the service of His Majesty as Governor and General of the said Armada to the discovery of the Isles of the West, and to keep to and comply with the said Instruction according to its contents, and of no other, and to perform well and faithfully the said office and charge of Governor and Captain-General, which in the name of the King Don Philip our Lord has been bestowed and ordained to him, and will pursue in all things his Royal service and the increase of his Patrimony and Royal Crown of Castile.'

Since Legazpi was ordered to keep the Instructions secret until the ships were 100 leagues out from Mexico, let us not pry into what they contained until then. Suffice it to say that the Almirante designate Juan Pablo de Carrion, who had wanted Urdaneta's opinion overruled, was ordered to stay behind, and so did. Urdaneta and the others concluded from this that they were going to New Guinea.

The time had now arrived for the concentration of the expedition's personnel at La Navidad. There were some 380 men in all. The crews numbered 150, there were 200 soldiers, 16 gentlemen, 6 Augustinian monks, 3 Crown officials and a scribe.

At Legazpi's side on the flagship *San Pedro* were his cousin Urdaneta, who was the Padre Prior or leader of the monks, and Legazpi's grandson Felipe de Salcedo. The chief pilot was Esteban Rodriguez, a loyal Spaniard, the intriguing Pierres Plun being second pilot on the flagship. On the *San Pedro* also was a company of 100 soldiers, commanded by Captain Martin de Goite, a fine soldier. In accordance with the custom of the time, a small company of gentlemen was attached to Legazpi as a personal retinue. Their 'duties' included the guarding of the Royal Standard.

On the other great galleon, the *San Pablo*, another soldier, Captain Mateo del Saz, was in command in place of Carrion, and was second-in-command of the whole expedition. With Saz was another company of 100 soldiers. The conspirators Jaymes Fortun, Juan Maria and Jorge the Greek were respectively the senior pilot, the master and the quartermaster of the *San Pablo*.

Legazpi's friend Juan de la Isla was the captain of the *San Juan*, of which his brother Rodrigo was pilot, and most of the officers were loyal Spaniards.

On the *San Lucas* Lope Martin remained as pilot, with his friend Juan Jañiz. At the last moment the captain designate, becoming unavailable through some misadventure, was replaced by one of Legazpi's company of gentlemen, Don Alonso de Arellano.

A supply of trading goods was brought from Mexico City under the personal supervision of the accountant, Andres de Cauchela, and loaded into the ships.

After the military had arrived in La Navidad, Pierres Plun, Lope Martin, Jaymes Fortun, Juan Maria, Jorge the Greek and the other sailors in the plot to seize the *San Lucas* found further allies in Juan Maria's friend Pablos Hernandez, a Venetian corporal, and some of his soldiers. Some forty sailors and soldiers in all were parties to the conspiracy. Yet no opportunity presented itself for the carrying out of their piratical design before the sailing of the expedition. This was not surprising, for in port the *San Lucas* was surrounded by the three other ships, and the conspirators themselves were scattered through them.

By no means, however, did this mean the end of the plot. The later confessions of some of the conspirators who were brought to justice, coupled with the sequence of events, show that Lope Martin of the *San Lucas*, Jaymes Fortun of the *San Pablo*, and their co-conspirators on those two vessels must have got their heads together on a variation of Plun's plan. Plun himself was pinned down on the *San Pedro*, but Lope Martin and Jaymes Fortun were in charge of the navigation of the *San Lucas* and the *San Pablo*. If therefore they could shake off the *San Pedro* and *San Juan* on the voyage by pretending they had been separated from them on a night when the sky was overcast, they could contrive that the *San Lucas* and the *San Pablo* should meet at dawn, and that they should in due course seize an opportunity to abscond with the *San Lucas*. Nor would there be any need for them to go to France as the French pilot Plun had suggested, since they could go to Italy or join the Portuguese after getting a valuable cargo in the Indies or Japan. Meanwhile the other ships would have gone to New Guinea.

The ceremonious Spaniards, on the eve of the departure, gathered all the personnel of the expedition together at a solemn ritual of swearing allegiance to God and the King of Spain. The immortal souls of Lope Martin and his fellow-conspirators were thus perjured before ever the Armada sailed.

On 20 November, 1564, Legazpi's four ships set sail from La Navidad, making a brave sight. The flagship *San Pedro* went under its mainsail and foresail, with the flag of Spain at the mast, and fired a salvo of farewell to the officials on shore. Behind it it towed a *fragata* – a decked pinnace – in which were four men. Then came the *San Pablo*. These two were the largest ships that had ever been in the South Sea up till that time. Then followed the *San Juan*, a midget compared with the big sailing ships, and finally the *San Lucas*, which was only half the size of the *San Juan*.

These ships had three masts and a steeply slanting bowsprit. The bowsprit was in fact a slanting mast for a spritsail hanging from a cross-arm, called picturesquely the *cebadura*, meaning 'nose-bag'. The main mast and the foremast carried square sails. The bonnets were extensions of the lower sails which could be fastened to their lower edges so as to hang down towards the deck. Finally there was the mizzenmast, a small mast towards the stern, on which a small fore-and-aft mizzensail could be mounted.

A hundred leagues out from Mexico, on 25 November, the Instructions from the Real Audiencia were opened by Legazpi. After reading them he called a meeting on the flagship attended by the captains, officials, monks and pilots of the expedition. At Legazpi's right hand was Captain Mateo del Saz, commander of the *San Pablo* and second-in-command of the expedition in place of Juan Pablo de Carrion, who after suggesting that the ships should go to the Philippines and not New Guinea had been ordered to stay behind. Andres de Urdaneta, who had no doubt that his advice that they should go to New Guinea was to be followed, was present with his fellow-churchmen. Juan de la Isla, captain of the *San Juan*, stood with Alonso de Arellano, captain of the *San Lucas*. The pilots, including the plotters Lope Martin of the *San Lucas* and Jaymes Fortun of the *San Pablo*, were also there.

The scribe, Hernan Riquel, now read to the company Legazpi's order embodying the Real Audiencia's decision on the destination of the Armada. Its primary objective was the Philippines!

2

Fly-by-Night

WHEN the Real Audiencia's decision was made known, Urdaneta and his ecclesiastical associates left no doubt of their views. Had they known before they left Mexico City that they were going elsewhere than New Guinea, they would not willingly have gone at all. They felt they had been deceived.

The procedures of the bureaucracy of Mexico City were certainly devious. Juan Pablo de Carrion had been removed from the expedition because of his differences with Urdaneta. Yet Carrion's opinion was in fact accepted. Valderrama and the magistrates evidently thought that if they divulged their decision before the ships were well out to sea, Urdaneta would probably withdraw, as he had said he would do if Carrion's opinion were followed. So they sacked Carrion, while conveying his view as an instruction to be kept secret until the ships were a hundred leagues off the coast.

Carrion was right in thinking that the Philippines were a more suitable centre for trade than New Guinea, although the main reason, namely that the Chinese junks which were in touch with the northern Philippines island of Luzon would take Mexican silver in exchange for their own profusion of wares was not clearly recognized for some time thereafter. Furthermore the Philippines were more conveniently placed for the return voyage to Mexico. It is hard to know what would have happened if the Spaniards had established themselves in New Guinea. Perhaps Australia would have become another Spanish empire. Perhaps the would-be settlers would have been decimated by the diseases of the area.

After the monks had had a little time to cool off, they accepted the situation with a good grace.

Urdaneta and his associates were not the only ones who found themselves somewhat taken aback when the decision to go to the Philippines was disclosed. Lope Martin and Jaymes Fortun, the pilots of the *San Lucas* and the *San Pablo*, no doubt had a furtive parley about the effect the decision might make on their own plan to abscond with the *San Lucas* to the Philippines in search of booty. The event showed, however, that they were determined to pursue their scheme. After all there were not only the Philippines, but Japan and China, as potential fields for their exploit.

Now the order in which the Armada was sailing at this time was first the *San Lucas*, which had been bidden to go ahead of the flagship *San Pedro*, as a scout at a distance of half a league, then the flagship itself, then the *San Pablo*, and finally the *San Juan*. In dark conditions at night the understanding was that a signal to shorten sail would be given by lantern from the flagship, whereupon the other ships would shorten sail also so as to keep together.

Lope Martin now started to take the *San Lucas* as far ahead of the flagship as two leagues when scouting for hidden dangers at night, so that if the sky became overcast he could the more easily fall off to leeward and dodge the flagship. When he was reminded from the flagship that his orders were to keep not more than half a league ahead, he answered that the *San Lucas* was low in the waist and shipped water in a cross-sea if he shortened sail too much. Lope Martin was never at a loss for a quick answer.

On the fifth evening after the meeting on the flagship, Lope Martin and Juan Jañiz on the *San Lucas*, and Jaymes Fortun, Juan Maria, Jorge the Greek and the other conspirators on the *San Pablo*, saw for the first time since leaving Mexico what they had been waiting for. The skies became overcast and rain began. As dark fell they looked towards the flagship for the expected signal to shorten sail. Surely enough, as the haze, rain and darkness deepened and it became increasingly difficult to see the lantern of the ship in front, the sails were reefed up on the flagship until she was going only on the foresail, while at the same time she showed the customary signal by lamp that the other ships should do the same.

Lope Martin on the *San Lucas* ahead of the flagship knew what he had to do, which was precisely nothing. He just kept on sailing the *San Lucas* into the gathering gloom. When the flagship and its lantern were out of sight, Martin let the ship run off course to leeward. He then raised the alarm by shouting that they had lost sight of the flagship in the rain and darkness. He blamed the low waist of the *San Lucas*, saying that when he saw the big ships shortening sail, he could not lose too much way himself, as otherwise they would have been swamped in the cross-seas. He said he would put a lantern at the stern as well as the mast and go as slowly as possible, keeping a watch for the other ships. But when morning came there was no sign of the other three ships, including the *San Pablo*.

Meanwhile on the *San Pablo*, as it followed behind the flagship, Jaymes Fortun the pilot, seeing the flagship shortening the mainsail and showing the customary signal, gave the order to shorten all sail. As the *San Pablo* lost way rapidly, it fell off to leeward. In a few moments the *San Pablo* would have parted from the other ships, with no overt evidence as to how this had happened. The early sailing

ships were always in danger of being parted in cross-winds
on dark nights even with the best of intentions.

Now the captain of the *San Pablo*, Mateo del Saz, was a
man of quick mind and resolute action, as befitted the
leading soldier of the expedition. He did not know much
about the sea or ships, but he did know the lantern of the
flagship was drawing away from them. He therefore ordered
the pilot and his mates to crack on more sail and keep the
flagship in sight, saying that if they lost it he would hang
them from the yard-arm.

Now it was obvious to Fortun and Maria and their fellow-
plotters that the captain was both willing and able to carry
out his threat, having a large number of soldiers on board
at his command. So they unfurled the sails again and kept the
flagship's lantern in sight.

Mateo del Saz did not then know the full extent of the
duplicity of Fortun and his cronies, although he was
sufficiently wary of them to hold the threat of death over
them for the rest of the voyage if they became separated from
the flagship. This, coupled with the disappearance of the
San Lucas itself, meant that the plan to seize the *San Lucas* had
failed. We shall see later that, nothing daunted, the conspirators on the *San Pablo* were to make the other small
vessel, the *San Juan*, the object of their piratical intentions,
although not on the voyage across the Pacific.

When dawn came without any sign of the *San Lucas*,
Legazpi's other ships resumed their course to the west,
hoping to see the missing vessel later in the prescribed route.
When they did not, the scribe noted in the official record
that Lope Martin was suspected of having separated from the
Armada deliberately, as indeed he had.

We shall leave the other three ships for a time and go
with the *San Lucas*, since it was a faster vessel than those
which remained with Legazpi. It had quite a trip.

In the absence of the *San Pablo* as well as the flagship and the *San Juan*, Lope Martin and Juan Jañiz had no recourse but to continue on for the Philippines as if the *San Lucas* really had been separated from the other ships by mischance. Since they did not know whether or not they had been betrayed by their fellow-plotters on the other ships, their obvious strategy was to try to keep out of the way of the Armada without raising the suspicions of the loyal Spaniards on board the *San Lucas*. As we have seen, the suspicion of wilful desertion was in fact noted in the official record on the flagship against Lope Martin, although not at that time against Arellano, the captain of the *San Lucas*. Later again, when it seemed inexplicable to Legazpi that if Arellano and his shipmates had in fact followed the prescribed route they would not have been met or heard of, he included Arellano in the charge of desertion. Suffice it here to say that, for reasons which will appear in due course when the charge is considered, the accusation against Arellano himself will not hold water.

At the time of the separation of the *San Lucas* from the other ships, at the beginning of December 1564, eleven days out from La Navidad, the Armada was proceeding west in an area of the Pacific where no islands lie ahead until the Marshalls, some three-fifths of the way to the Philippines from Mexico. Neither the people of the *San Lucas* nor of the main ships had any idea of the tremendous distances that were involved in this passage. They knew, however, that Villalobos, over twenty years previously, had after many weeks encountered one lot of islands in latitude nine degrees north, and then another lot in ten degrees. These two groups of islands were in fact in the Marshalls and the western Carolines. A glance at the map of the Pacific area will show the geography.

Arellano and Lope Martin, having proceeded west in nine degrees for some weeks, concluded they must have missed Villalobos's islands in nine degrees, and therefore shifted their latitude to ten degrees in the hope of picking up the second group. The truth was, however, that they were still well short of the Marshalls.

Some five weeks after the separation from the other ships, and 41 days out from Mexico, the *San Lucas* was sailing before a stiff wind in latitude 10¼ degrees when suddenly land and breakers showed up right ahead.

Lope Martin gave a quick order to haul the starboard bowlines and put the helm over, hoping that by thus going to starboard close-hauled he would be making the best guess for clearing the danger ahead. They passed some rocks with the side of the ship scraping against them. The sailors then called on Our Lady of Consolation of Guadelupe to deliver them, for they found themselves confronted by a reef which it was impossible to avoid.

Lope shouted out the order to shorten foresail. He wanted to lose way preparatory to grounding the vessel at a spot he could see ahead where there were not so many breakers on the reef. As he ran to the prow a sea came over the low waist of the ship and carried him over the side. With one hand Lope caught hold of a ship's rope, and as he fell he saw the rocks so close at hand that he could see that the ship was already over them. It was generally agreed that the ship and Lope himself had been saved only by prayer.

They stood off until morning, and then found that the land was so low that it scarcely appeared above the sea. They coasted it and found that there were some 36 islets arranged in a triangle running from north-west to south-east, surrounded by a reef through which they could find no entrance, and with no sign of habitation. They could not get bottom for anchorage, and therefore sailed on.

This was Likiep Atoll in the Marshalls. The *San Lucas*, coming across the Pacific in about the tenth parallel of latitude, had struck the heart of this remote group.

The next day the *San Lucas* came to some more islets about 100 miles from Likiep, in latitude nine degrees. They were part of Kwajalein Atoll. Here they found an insecure anchorage. Along came a native sailing canoe in which were two men and a boy, whom the European visitors persuaded to come aboard, giving them some beads and a knife and some toy bells, and to the boy a shirt. In return the islanders gave them some fish and coconuts and water which were in the canoe. The ship's boat was got out, and Arellano and Martin, with eight men, accompanied the canoe to a nearby island where there were some huts. Here the Spaniards met the wives of their hosts, and two babies. The ladies wore palm petticoats, the men nothing. They were poor fisherfolk who lived on what they could get from the sea, and on the coconuts that abounded on the atoll. They appeared to be the only people in that part of the atoll, and were merely temporary visitors, indicating by signs that their home was elsewhere. They gave the Europeans some coconuts, and as night was coming on the ship's boat returned to the ship.

The next day the ship sighted a low, compact, well-peopled small island, in latitude 8½ degrees. It was lower in the middle than on the coast, and the ship's company were surprised to find when they got close to it that its inner parts were plentifully wooded with palms, which could not be seen at a distance from the sea. They could not find anchorage, and the people, some of whom swam out to the ship, were well armed and numerous, so they did not try to make a landing. This was Lib.

The *San Lucas* had now passed through the Marshalls. In doing so it had decreased the latitude from 10 to 8½ degrees, having come sharply south-west of Likiep. From Lib the

ship continued to decrease the latitude by another degree.
Why should this marked change of course have been made?
It is hard to avoid the conclusion that this was part of Lope
Martin's strategy to avoid the probable course of the other
ships of the expedition. However that might be, the effect
was to put the *San Lucas* in latitudes well to the south of
those of other European voyages across the North Pacific
both before and after for a very long period, the result being
that Arellano and Lope Martin became the first European
discoverers of a number of interesting islands in the Caroline
group.

Continuing on to the west, and narrowly escaping a reef
one night on the way, the ship came, on 17 January, to
some islands in 7½ degrees which, from the descriptions,
were unmistakably those of Truk, the largest atoll in the
Caroline group. There were a number of high islands in a
very large lagoon, surrounded by a reef on which were
strung a number of low islets.

Coming into the lagoon through the eastern entrance, the
San Lucas was received by a number of canoes from the
nearest island, Toloas, and began at their invitation to enter
the inlet in Toloas known today as Dublon. One of the
islanders was showing the pilot the way. But the wind was
adverse, and great numbers of canoes from the surrounding
islands, full of men armed with lances, clubs and slings,
bore down on the ship. So the *San Lucas* drew off, and started
on a perilous course across the lagoon among the reefs with
which it was strewn, seeking an outlet through the surrounding reef.

As the ship was picking its way in this fashion, some canoes
came up to the ship's boat at the stern with the obvious
intention of making off with it. Arellano told two of his
men to get into the boat to defend it. One of the assailants
in the bow of one of the canoes tried to kill one of these men

with a blow from a club, but the soldier defended himself with much spirit. Then the warriors in the canoes began to throw spears at the Spaniards on the ship from all directions. Many of these stuck in the deck, and it was a wonder nobody on board was killed. So Arellano ordered a volley to be fired by the musketeers to frighten the canoes off. This had the desired effect, and the canoes fled amid much shouting to their islands.

Night was now coming on, and the ship's company were in a desperate position, being trapped in the reef-studded lagoon with a stiff wind blowing, and without being able to find firm bottom to anchor.

Arellano and Lope Martin peered ahead into the gathering gloom. Arellano asked if it were any use turning back. Martin replied that they could never make the eastern exit in the dark. Their only hope was to put in the night somehow out in the broad expanse of the lagoon.

As dark fell, many fires sprang up on the islands in the lagoon, and the sound of much shouting from the excited inhabitants could be heard.

As the ship moved slowly over the lagoon, while the people on board peered vainly at the leadsman for a sign that he had found good bottom, white water indicating a shoal where they might find firm anchorage was seen at a distance. Martin took a bearing on it with his compass, so that after dark finally fell he might be able to keep a course on the shoal after losing sight of it.

They crept ahead in this fashion, being obliged to keep a moderate amount of way on the vessel in order to hold the course. The leadsman found no bottom for so long a time that they thought they must have missed the shoal. On all sides they could hear the sea breaking on the reefs.

Suddenly the leadsman, peering at the line with his lantern, shouted that he had bottom in thirty fathoms.

They threw out a grapnel. When it engaged with the
bottom it began to drag, for the part where it had struck
was live rock. They threw out the heavy anchor because it
was their only hope. The cable tautened. Would the anchor
drag too? The pilot thought the ship was moving. But it
proved to be merely swinging with the wind, and the anchor
held.

The company of the *San Lucas* had escaped a natural
menace for a time. There was still, however, the menace
from the islands to be faced when day dawned. Pedro de
Rivero, Arellano's second-in-command, put extra men on
watch and prepared for the expected attack in the morning.
They loaded some of the culverins with pebbles, and put
lead in others. They were in fact ill-prepared for war, with
little ammunition. Furthermore they were worn out through
poor food and the heavy toil and stresses of the previous day.

When day broke they were relieved to find that no canoes
could be seen coming to attack them at that time. They
spread some sail and upped anchor with much groaning
from the tired sailors, and once again began to thread their
way past the islands and reefs in the western part of the
lagoon. At one point they passed over a reef which had little
more water over it than the depth of the vessel itself.

They were passing beyond the last of the islands in the
lagoon when ten or twelve canoes came out from it, inviting the ship by signs to go to the island, where they would
get food and water. When the canoes got nearer, however,
it was seen that the people in them were plainly preparing to
attack.

A sailor who fancied his skill as a gunner asked Arellano to
let him fire some of the stone-shot. Arellano gave his consent
and the sailor manoeuvred one of the culverins until its
muzzle was aligned on a large canoe in the forefront of the
native craft. The fuse was touched off and the gunpowder

exploded with a roar. So good, or so lucky, was the aim that the stones struck inside the canoe, doing great havoc. All the people in it flung themselves into the water with much yelling to the other canoes, the occupants of which were astonished both at the noise of the gun and its result.

The gunner asked to be allowed to repeat his feat, but Arellano would not allow it, and indeed it was unnecessary. The islanders desisted from their attack while the vessel sailed past them.

The *San Lucas* then went through the western pass out of the lagoon of Truk into the open sea beyond. It was the first European vessel to make contact with that highly interesting island cluster, which was not rediscovered for more than two centuries thereafter.

The origin and structure of the Micronesian islands which were encountered by the various ships of Legazpi's expedition is fascinating in itself. They are all remnants of ancient outpourings of basaltic lava from the ocean floor, which raised their heads above sea-level as active volcanoes, in due course became extinct, and were wholly or partially eroded. Then the coral polyp built its wonderful masonry on the parts of these volcanic remnants lying just below the level of the sea. The lagoons and their surrounding reefs are the ancient craters and hollows in the coral-covered basalt.

The morning after the *San Lucas* left Truk, three small islets disposed in a triangle on the reef surrounding the inner lagoon were found. These were the islands of Pulap Atoll in the Carolines – another new discovery. Water and wood were badly needed, so the *San Lucas* anchored close to one of the islands.

On the beach were a large number of warriors armed with the usual spears, clubs and slings. Some canoes came out, and the people of the *San Lucas* dropped some gifts down to them from the ship. Thus encouraged, two chiefs came on

B

board, and were made to understand that wood and water were desired.

A young sailor now undertook to go to the shore for water. He got into one of the canoes with some water-jars and, greatly daring, went ashore with the islanders alone. In due course he came back in the canoe with his new-found friends, bringing a jar of water, a bunch of green bananas and some fermented coconut milk. When the lad was back on board, well pleased with himself, he reported that the island was a fine spot and that the people were friendly.

The ship's boat was now launched to go for wood and water in quantity. Arellano and Lope Martin, with a crew of eight, made for the shore, with the chiefs in their canoes going as guides in front. The canoes went through an opening in the reef to the beach, beckoning to the boat to come in.

Arellano and Martin discussed whether they should accept the invitation. They agreed that whereas the canoes drew little water the reef could rip the bottom out of the boat in no time, particularly when it was loaded with wood and water. Furthermore they did not like what they saw on shore, where the warriors had divided, some of them going off and taking cover behind the trees with their spears ready.

The boat accordingly returned to the ship, followed by some islanders, several of whom came on board. Again these visitors made signs inviting Arellano to send some men ashore for wood and water.

The young sailor who had gone ashore before volunteered again. He therefore got into one of the visiting canoes with some jars. Another sailor followed his example and got into a second canoe, which started after the first canoe. A third sailor followed in a third canoe.

The first sailor was taken ashore by the islanders and disembarked with his jars. The second sailor came ashore fast on his heels. The third canoe was approaching the opening in the reef when the sailor in it was horrified to see the first lad running desperately towards the beach pursued by a number of men with clubs. They seized and clubbed both him and the second sailor at the water's edge, and dragged their bodies away.

Seeing these things happen, the third sailor signed violently to the islanders who were taking him ashore to turn round and go back to the ship, but they took no notice and kept on towards the land. The frantic sailor yelled out at the uncomprehending canoemen, who were obviously determined in any case to take him to a fate similar to that which had just overtaken his friends.

The sailor now seized the paddle from the hands of the nearest native to him and worked furiously to turn the canoe around. As he tried to do so one of the men hit him on the head with a club, and the others came at him with their clubs to finish him off. But he pulled a dagger out of his belt and stabbed and killed two of his assailants, while the other jumped into the water. The sailor was thus left alone in the canoe, while a rain of stones was flung at him from slings on shore and from other canoes which were making for him.

The people on the ship, when they saw these things happening to the sailor, went to seize two islanders who were still on board, but these men jumped into the water and swam like fish for the shore. Some of the ship's company, jumping into the boat, started rowing furiously after the swimmers and to the rescue of their sorely pressed shipmate. Seeing that the swimmers could not be overtaken before they reached the reef, a musketeer in the boat shot and killed one of them.

The sailor in the canoe, badly battered by the clubs and stones with which he had been assailed, was taken back to the ship.

Arellano now determined to avenge the deaths of the two
sailors, calling on a landing-party to go with him against the
islanders, even if it meant death for themselves. The boat was
accordingly manned and went round the reef looking for a
safe place where they could go in, while a constant rain of
stones came from the island. So good were the slingers that
some of the stones nearly reached the ship at its anchorage well
off shore. But the boat could not get in to the shore without
the greatest peril of being lost on the rocks, and had to
return to the ship.

For two centuries thereafter the old Spanish sea-charts of
the North Pacific bore a vague name Los Martyres – The
Martyrs – commemorating the two sailor-lads who lost their
lives on an unknown island in the vast expanses of the Great
Ocean so long ago.

The frequent warfare in the Carolines could not fail to
make the islanders suspicious of strangers and quick to take
advantage of them. The Europeans of the *San Lucas* must have
appeared no less alien to the dusky islanders of Pulap than
they themselves did to the Europeans.

When the *San Lucas* left Mexico her personnel numbered
ten crewmen as well as ten soldiers. The calamity at Pulap
reduced her experienced sailors to eight, which was little
enough for the working of a three-masted sailing ship.

The *San Lucas*, after leaving Pulap, resumed her course
towards the west. Arellano and Martin had no idea how far
they still were from the Philippines, and expected to see
them at any time. They increased their latitude towards the
north in order to make the Philippines in nine degrees.

A few days after leaving Pulap, the *San Lucas* came to
another small island, with some sand-keys near it. It seemed
at first to be uninhabited, but then a fire was seen, and some
islanders came down to the beach. The ship passed on to one
of the sand-keys, the Europeans being now wary of islanders
on beaches.

This was Sorol, another of the Caroline atolls, and another fresh discovery by Arellano and Lope Martin.

After a time two sailing canoes came from the shore of the main islet towards the ship, the people in them copper-hued with black hair, like the inhabitants of the other islands of Micronesia. In their hands they bore the customary Micronesian weapons, the spear, club and sling.

Lope Martin dropped a red jacket in the water alongside the ship and made signs to the canoemen to take it. One of the canoes drew alongside to pick it up. The people of the *San Lucas* waited with a culverin loaded with stones, and with arquebuses ready. As the canoe came past the side of the ship one of the soldiers leaned over, grabbed a youth in the canoe by the hair, and yanked him over the low side of the ship by main force on to the deck. At the same time the muskets were fired point-blank at the canoe near the ship and the culverin at the other canoe. The islanders, some wounded, all jumped into the sea and swam ashore. The Spaniards seized the canoes to make firewood.

The captured youth of Sorol had his long hair cut, was given breeches and shirt to cover his nakedness, and received the name of Vicente because his capture took place on Saint Vincent's Day.

From Sorol the ship proceeded on, seeing Ngulu from a distance one evening. Some days later, on 29 January, 1565, the high land of Mindanao, the southern island of the Philippines, hove in sight.

Almost as soon as the mountains of Mindanao were clearly visible, the *San Lucas* was in trouble again. The sun was already setting, and the wind blew so briskly from the sea to the land that it drove them swiftly towards a lee shore.

The boat's crew prepared to launch the boat in order to try to hold the ship off shore by towing it. The crew had the greatest difficulty in getting the boat out and away, because the great waves which were driving against it threatened to smash the boat and the crew too. Having got it clear, the rowers tried to hold the ship off the land, but slowly the seas got the better of them. Dark fell, and at 2 o'clock in the morning the pilot at the mast could see the indistinct whiteness of the surf on shore.

The pilot then came down from the crow's nest and asked the master, Nicolas the Greek, who was a skilled carpenter, to knock some planks together into a raft so that if they had to take to the boat they could tow the raft with some food and equipment on it.

The master and some helpers started to do this, but even as they were feverishly nailing the planks together, the wind from the sea began to change to a breeze from the land. With it came a sweet smell from the luxuriant Philippines, which lifted their spirits so that their past travail seemed as nothing. The ship steadily came away from the land, and thanks were given to the Lady of Consolation of Guadelupe for saving them yet once more.

The pilot now spread his chart and invited Arellano to examine it. He pointed out the position of Davao Gulf, the main port of Mindanao, not far to the south of the latitude of nine degrees in which they had struck the east coast of Mindanao. These waters were known from the visit of Villalobos. Martin pointed out how the seas were running to the south along the coast. Villalobos could not get a northing against them, and neither could the *San Lucas*. It was agreed that they should run down the coast to Davao.

On 30 January, 1565, the *San Lucas* found safe anchorage in Davao Gulf. She was 8000 miles and 71 days out from Mexico, during which time her company had discovered a number of islands and had had enough excitement for twenty voyages.

3

Pacific Odyssey

AFTER the *San Lucas* had come to anchor in a cove inside the mouth of Davao Gulf, Captain Arellano ordered a volley to be fired. No Filipinos, however, showed up at this time, rather to the relief of the ship's company after their terrifying experiences at previous islands in the Carolines.

Don Pedro de Rivero, the second-in-command, now went in the ship's boat with six or seven soldiers and sailors to the land, where a stream of water was found. Seven or eight barrels of water were got aboard that day, and also some firewood. The voyagers felt their spirits and strength coming back in the beautiful, sweet-smelling haven.

The next morning the people of the *San Lucas* heard shouting from the land. Two or three men up on the slope of the hill opposite the anchorage were working their way down through the jungle towards the beach, calling out as they went. The men soon appeared on the beach near the ship, and beckoned to the people on board.

Pilot Lope Martin got into the ship's boat with a few men and went to the land. As he approached he could see that the men wore cloth head-coverings and breeches with daggers in the belts, giving a very different appearance from the naked warriors of the Carolines. Furthermore it was plain from their reactions that they had seen European ships before and were disposed to trade. They made signs to

Martin that they would be back, and then went off over the hill again. Martin then returned to the ship.

Before long thirty or forty men, led by a finely dressed chief, appeared on the shore and beckoned to the ship. Arellano and Martin got into the boat with a small party of supporters and made for the beach.

As the Europeans reached the edge of the water, the chief waded in and, taking a little water in his hand, crossed himself. This was no doubt the result of contact with the Portuguese in the Moluccas, to the south-east of Mindanao.

Arellano and Martin now jumped out and exchanged embraces with the chief, with much enthusiasm on both sides. Then the chief, to confirm the friendly relations, took out the fine dagger which he wore in his belt and showed by signs that he wanted to prick some blood from his chest according to the Philippine custom of showing friendship.

But Arellano made signs in token of dissuasion, whereupon the chief accepted that the ceremony be dispensed with.

The chief, who gave his name as Viban, and who seemed to be no more than twenty years of age, now signed to the visitors to sit down, and when they had done so some attendants brought some canes full of a sort of wine. Viban first drank some of the wine to show that it was good, and then handed it to Arellano and Martin. It proved to be a highly agreeable sweet wine, with the hue and taste of cinnamon combined with ginger. The visitors thus had their first direct experience of some of the spices which were one of the main objectives of the Europeans in their probes of the Indies.

Gifts were now exchanged, the chief being particularly pleased with a piece of iron. Then they parted for the night, the Filipinos returning to their village at some distance from the anchorage of the *San Lucas*, Arellano and his companions to the ship.

The next day Viban came back with more than two hundred followers, bearing pigs, fowls, small fox-like dogs killed for food, rice, yams, honey, wax, sugarcane as thick as a man's arm and a fathom long, incense, many canes of the cinnamon and ginger wine, oranges, lemons and plantains of three different sorts. They also had many fine porcelain pots, painted in various designs, which like their ironware were in fact of Chinese origin. The earthenware of these pots was so hard that Arellano found it would cut a nail as with a file.

Viban now signed to Arellano and his little retinue to sit down, and trading began. The Filipinos showed themselves to be good bargainers, and to be mainly interested in iron, so the Spaniards concentrated their purchases on much-needed food.

The next day Viban came again, this time with his brother and two other chiefs, accompanied with their wives, who were attended by some girls. The ladies were very fine-looking, and wore long skirts, elegant bodices, and on their heads handsome bonnets rather in the manner of the peasant women of Spain. In return the women showed much interest in the appearance of the Westerners, who gave them gifts of fine cloth. The women then returned to their village. Again a feast was held, the chief item being baked pig. Arellano, Rivero and Martin were each given a many-tinted palm helmet by the chiefs. Then more trading took place, quantities of food and wine being bought by the Spaniards.

In the days that followed, it was seldom that there were not some ten or a dozen of the people of Davao Gulf on the shore near the ship. From time to time they showed signs of not being entirely reliable. During this time water and wood in quantity were secured for the ship.

Twenty-five days passed, and no sign of Legazpi and his ships appeared. No doubt this caused Lope Martin and his

friend Jañiz no great grief, for they were unsure of their
reception if and when they rejoined Legazpi. For this feeling
there was good reason, since Lope Martin was in fact
suspected by Legazpi of having engineered the desertion of
the *San Lucas* from the fleet.

Arellano and Lope Martin now decided to fill in the time
by doing some repairs to the *San Lucas* and building up its
topsides.

One day Lope Martin was on land with the master,
Nicolas the Greek, and four sailors, cutting timber for the
work on the ship. Nicolas then took the opportunity of
having some conversation with Lope. He said that he and
the other four sailors who were with him were sick of
cutting wood when they knew that there were native craft
in the Philippines and nearby Moluccas plying back and forth
with gold and spices. They wanted to know if Lope would
be with them in a plot to seize control of the *San Lucas* and
make themselves rich by raiding these vessels.

Lope Martin, whose experience in intrigue was a deal
ahead of that of the Greek, gave a somewhat scornful reply.
The party returned to the ship with considerable ill-will as
between Martin and the conspirators, who feared that
Martin might betray them.

As soon as he had an opportunity, Lope reported the conversation to Arellano, saying that he would attempt to
dissuade the master from making mischief because it was
very important that, with only eight crewmen including
himself, diplomacy should be used.

That night Arellano and Martin each took a turn on watch.
During the pilot's watch the master himself approached him,
saying that he had thought better of what he had proposed
that afternoon. Martin assured Nicolas that Arellano knew
about the matter but was willing to forget it if Nicolas

behaved himself. Soon afterwards Arellano came up on deck and peace was confirmed with the master.

While these parleys were going forward, the four sailors with whom Nicolas had plotted perceived that he was going back on the conspiracy, and became alarmed at their own position. They quietly took some arquebuses and other gear, including both of the ship's flints for making fire, slipped into the ship's boat, and cast off. Too late the watch raised the alarm. A rush was made to the side, but the sailors had gone. They were seen heading for the mouth of the Gulf, although just what plan they might be working to was not clear. It seemed possible they had it in mind to make for the Moluccas.

Great was the consternation on the *San Lucas* over this defection. Not only was the boat essential for getting adequate food and water, and for towing the ship's head round in narrow waters, but the removal of both the ship's steels left them without the means of making fire for the guns and muskets and for domestic purposes. Furthermore the deserters themselves formed half of the experienced working force of the ship.

In the morning Rivero, who was much respected by all the ship's company, volunteered to go ashore and follow the coast to the entrance to the Gulf in the hope of finding the boat and persuading the sailors to return on the promise of pardon.

In the absence of the boat the ship came in as close to land as possible. Rivero and two soldiers leapt ashore through the surf and made a long tramp to the head of the port, but came back without seeing any sign of the boat. All the time they were on land they had the fear of being ambushed and cut off by the inhabitants. Another anxiety arose when the ship, as the result of coming close to the shore, got stuck for a while, being eventually floated off by the rising tide.

Now the four deserters were simple sailormen who had
been first led astray by Nicolas the Greek and then, as they
thought, betrayed by him. It was not long before they
repented of going outside the Gulf. They had hopes that
some of their friends on board might support them. So on
the third day they were seen to come back into the cove
where the ship was anchored off shore, and to pitch their
small tent near a stream.

The pilot now swam ashore with a rope tied to his waist.
Coming within earshot of the rebels, he tried every artifice
and appeal that his glib tongue could summon to get them to
capitulate. He asked them how they could think of leaving
the King's service so disloyally and stealing his boat, thereby
denying the duty they owed to Christ. Furthermore the
natives would certainly slay them if they remained there.

To this the sailors replied that if they gave themselves up
they would have no chance anyway, but would be executed
for desertion. Martin assured them that the captain had
already pardoned Nicolas and offered them also a pardon if
they came back. But despite Martin's entreaties they remained unpersuaded.

The pilot then returned to the ship, not without further
anxious moments when the vessel, in coming near the shore,
touched ground. When Lope was on board again he reported
that the only hope appeared to be for the captain to go ashore
himself and assure the rebels that they would get amnesty if
they returned.

Arellano and Martin accordingly both made the perilous
journey through the breakers over the reefs to the shore.
When they got ashore they found that the four sailors had
gone a short distance out from the beach in the boat as a
precaution against them.

Arellano called out to them from the shore, beseeching
them as loyal men and Christians to come back, and giving
his word as a Christian that they would come to no harm.

To this appeal, however, the soldiers again returned a firm no, thinking no doubt that if Arellano did not string them up someone else would sooner or later as mutineers.

Arellano then tried another line, pleading with the sailors to return the boat at least, pointing out to them that if they kept it they would be condemning everybody on board the ship to death, including their friends and shipmates.

The mutineers had a short consultation and then spoke from the boat to Arellano on shore.

They said they would not give themselves up on any account, but did not wish to keep the boat at the risk of the lives of their shipmates on the *San Lucas*. Provided therefore Rivero came ashore with no more than two men to row the boat back, they would give it up to him.

Arellano asked that they also give Rivero one of the steels, and the muskets they had taken.

Arellano and Martin now made their way back to the ship. As they did so Arellano struck his head against a rock which lay in his way as he was swimming. This was not calculated to make the deserters any more popular with him.

It was now Rivero's turn to go in through the surf to the shore, accompanied by two men. To the unspeakable joy of the ship's company, he was in due course seen returning in the boat. With him he brought one of the steels, but not the muskets, which the recalcitrant sailors retained for their own protection.

That evening the pilot was by no means easy in his mind. He told Arellano he did not like leaving the sailors, since he needed them, and that furthermore if they were not secured soon they were liable to be killed by the Filipinos.

They looked ashore to where the deserters were camped, seeing clearly their tent in the light of their fire. Two of them could be seen keeping watch with muskets, the other two being evidently in the tent.

Martin then suggested that since they now had the boat, they should take a party and land down the coast a bit where they could not be seen. They might then be able to creep round the slope behind the deserters and take them by surprise.

The stratagam was agreed on accordingly. Rivero remained in charge of the ship, and Arellano and Martin, with Bo'sun Moreto and a sailor whom they could trust, went ashore with three soldiers.

When the landing-party reached the shore some distance away from the objective, Moreto and the sailor were left in charge of the ship's boat with instructions to come quickly if they heard a shot. The five others then began to work their way up through the forested slopes and round behind the deserters' camp. It was tough going, through ravines and over ridges, but eventually they came out on a flat beside the stream which flowed past the camp. They followed it down through the trees, and eventually picked up the path running from the stream to the camp.

As the stalkers stealthily approached the fire, they could clearly see the two men on watch with their arquebuses at the ready. One of them in particular was keeping a constant watch, and Arellano and his party settled down silently, awaiting a convenient opportunity.

Two hours went by, and then one of the watchers went to get the other two to take their turn on guard. Only one of them, however, came out of the tent, the other having reneged on his watch. Only one man was therefore now on watch. He also was particularly conscientious, walking round peering from side to side, but the night was dark and the ambushers remained undiscovered. Since their idea was to capture the men unharmed, the assailants held their fire.

Now Lope Martin was not a patient man. As time went on in this fashion, his forbearance wore thin. Eventually the guard had to put some wood on the fire, and Lope, as soon as the watcher relaxed his attention, fired a charge of twenty-seven pellets from his musket almost point-blank at the man's chest.

Here came a miracle, as they agreed afterwards when the facts were known. A sacred image hung from the man's neck. Some of the pellets lodged in the man's chest round the image, but the image itself took most of the charge, thereby undoubtedly saving the sailor's life.

Lope now pursued his wounded victim with a sword, while Arellano called on the other three men, as they rushed out of the tent, to surrender. They showed fight and were not subdued without being wounded. Finally the four of them were bound and bundled into the boat which Moreto had brought to the beach nearby. Then captors and captives returned to the *San Lucas*.

The incorrigible spirit which had been shown by the four sailors had greatly incensed Arellano. He ordered that halters be got ready to hang them. Rivero then interceded for the men. Lope Martin raised his voice too, saying they needed the men even to get the ship out of the Gulf.

Arellano therefore agreed to reprieve the culprits, saying he would deliver them to the judgment of Legazpi when the Armada was found. Before long, however, the men were fully restored to Arellano's good graces by their good conduct and remorse.

The repairs to the ship were now proceeded with, and crosses of timber, with bottles at the feet containing messages, were put in conspicuous places to attract the attention of Legazpi's ships if they came.

Viban, with his lesser chiefs and their wives, now once more visited the cove where the *San Lucas* was anchored. Their foreheads and noses were smeared with a sweet-smelling unguent, and they wore gold ornaments, the metal for which they said came from mines in the interior of Mindanao. Viban said he was going off on a hunting trip, and returned in a few days with some trophies of the chase. Then Viban went off again, the Spaniards being told that he had gone on another hunting trip.

The next night, the watch on deck suddenly gave the alarm. The Spaniards had placed some of the dogs they had got from the local traders so that their barking would warn the watch of anybody approaching the anchorage along the beach. These dogs had been aroused, and it was plain that a number of people were on the shore. The suspicions of the people on the *San Lucas* were confirmed when three large canoes could be seen in the offing, creeping towards the ship.

Immediately the ship's company manned the guns and the arquebuses were got out.

The indications that the *San Lucas* had been alerted were apparently seen by the canoes, for they changed course and disappeared behind a point of land. It was agreed that the canoes had aimed to cut the ship's cables so that it would go ashore, whereupon the people on shore and in the canoes would have had the small company of the *San Lucas* at their mercy.

Next morning the canoes which had withdrawn behind the point of land were seen issuing forth and approaching the ship. To the sorrow of the Europeans, in one of them was their erstwhile friend Viban. With him was an older chief to whom Viban appeared to pay deference.

Viban was indeed on a hunting trip.

It was now decided that it was high time for the *San Lucas* to put to sea. The sails were accordingly spread, and the ship sailed out of Davao Gulf. On 4 March, 1565, the *San Lucas* thus began the second part of one of the greatest voyages in the history of the sea.

By this time Arellano had a well-founded admiration for

Lope Martin's nerve and seamanship, and a close association had grown between them.

The *San Lucas* first came down to the small island of Sarangani, near the south-east extremity of Mindanao. Still seeing no sign of Legazpi, they decided to sail round the south and west sides of Mindanao and so work their way north through the Philippines.

On the south coast of Mindanao, the *San Lucas* stayed for several days in a bay, taking in water. Here Arellano and Martin went ashore with two dogs and did some hunting, managing to kill a stag, and seeing many pigs and fowls.

Farther on along the south coast, a very large native vessel was seen. When the *San Lucas* approached it, a shower of lances and arrows was launched at the ship. One of the *San Lucas's* culverins was fired and hit the craft squarely, with the result that the steersman gave up his post and the vessel broached sideways on to the seas. Coming close, Arellano ordered another culverin to be fired, whereupon the people in the vessel, numbering about 150, all jumped into the water.

When a boarding-party searched the vessel, they found much rice and produce, and also some pieces of gold. After taking some of the food, the Europeans left the vessel to its owners and proceeded on their way.

The *San Lucas* worked its way round the south-western extremity of Mindanao. In the islands near Zamboanga, they saw many native vessels, buying some fish from them to eke out their food supplies. (The double outriggers of Zamboanga still make a brave sight as they sail to and from the pearl fisheries today.)

Having come up the west side of Mindanao, the *San Lucas* eventually came in sight of its northern coast. The last contact of the company of the *San Lucas* with the soil of Mindanao before they sailed away from it towards the islands to the north was another memorable occasion. At a cove where the ship's boat was loading water and wood, the master, Nicolas the Greek, came to Arellano. He said that all the ship's company were in need of having their clothes washed in fresh water. He proposed therefore that he should go ashore with two lads who could wash the clothes while the boat was fetching the water and wood.

The two lads were engaged in washing the clothes of the entire company in a stream on shore when a crowd of islanders burst out of the trees at a distance from the beach, armed with lances and swords.

The master, seeing the danger, yelled to the launderers to run for the shore, and the ship's boat came to their aid. The master himself grabbed some of the clothing, and started towards the surf. The yelling warriors were breathing down his neck as, encumbered with the clothing, he struggled through the breakers. A lance hit him, and then another, while the foremost of his assailants gave him a cut with a sword. He dropped the clothing and was rescued in the nick of time.

The master received nine wounds in all, but survived. For the rest of the voyage the ship's company had little more than the clothes they stood up in.

The *San Lucas* now stood over from the north-western extremity of Mindanao for Zebu, about 50 miles to the north. It was at Zebu and the nearby Mactan that Magellan and a number of his associates had been killed.

The *San Lucas* was now in the very heart of the Philippines, and as the ship approached Zebu, a magnificent panorama of islands could be seen on all sides.

East of Zebu at a short distance is the island of Bohol. At the very time when the San Lucas passed between the two islands, Legazpi's galleons were anchored in an inlet on the south-west side of Bohol.

The *San Lucas* now came into the shallow waters north of Bohol, full of small islands, shoals and treacherous currents. The passage through the inner sea of the Philippines between Zebu, Bohol and Leyte was now to test the skill of Lope Martin to the utmost.

At one point they came suddenly on a shoal. 'Haul the bowlines,' ordered Martin, the effect being to bring the ship close to the wind in an endeavour to skirt the shoal. Then, seeing that they were in real bother with shallows all around, Martin gave another quick order to let the anchor go, the sails being still up. The anchor landed on a reef so close alongside the ship that the stock of the anchor still showed above the water. 'Shorten courses', yelled the pilot. The mainsail and foresail were furled up accordingly. The ship, losing all way, was then swung by the current and began to bump against the reef. Seeing that the only hope was to keep way on, the pilot ordered the foresail to be unfurled again, and the anchor to be weighed. The ship began to move against the current with the foresail, but the current kept swinging the bow onto the reef, and they could not get it on to the other tack. So the pilot ordered two men to go out on to the prow with the yard of the spritsail and try to push the ship round. This manoeuvre worked, and the ship sailed away from the reef over the shallows into deeper water.

The *San Lucas* coasted Leyte, to the north-east of Zebu, and so came into deep water among high islands. On the coasts they saw many villages, with much fertile country, and high mountains inland.

The ship then passed through San Bernardino Strait and the islands north of Samar, fighting currents in some places, riding them in others. At one point they passed a large sailing canoe, the crew of which called out 'Capitan' and 'Pilote', showing no doubt that they had had some contact with the Portuguese.

Eventually the *San Lucas* was clear of the Philippines with open sea on each hand and ahead. It was Easter Eve, 21 April, 1565.

Arellano and Lope Martin now had a conference. They had not seen any trace of the Armada, said Arellano, despite having traversed the Philippines. To go back among the islands would be suicide. The Portuguese had dominion over the route to the west and the islands to the south of the Philippines, and the King of Spain's orders were to stay out of Portuguese waters.

Martin himself had no doubt of what they should do, namely try to strike to the north-east and see if they could sail in high latitudes to Mexico. He thought that seasonal winds from the south-west would be blowing before long. It was accordingly agreed that this was their best course.

When the news was given out to the ship's company, there was some dissatisfaction. It was said that New Spain was 2000 leagues away, whereas the Portuguese in the Moluccas were near at hand, and that the ships that had preceded them in the attempt to sail back east to New Spain had all failed. But Arellano and Lope Martin stood firm on their decision, so the company of the *San Lucas* commended themselves to God and set sail on Easter Day, 22 April, 1565.

Picking up helpful winds, the *San Lucas* forged her way towards the north-east. The pilot kept marking his calculated positions on his chart, showing Arellano where they were aiming for. He explained that they would pass close by 'Pago'. Marco Polo would scarcely have recognized the cartographers' mutilation of his 'Zipango', namely Japan.

Rivero now went below decks with the steward to take account of the food and water. There were eight barrels of water, each about three-quarters full, twenty quintals of broken biscuit, some beans and some chick-peas. When this was reported to Arellano, he gave the command that the

water and food be strictly rationed, and that when supplies
were drawn one of the senior officers should be present.

Slowly Lope's points on the chart crept towards the 30th
parallel, close to where Japan was thought to be. In 31
degrees they came on a small, very high crag rising straight
out of the sea. This must have been one of the volcanic
islands to the south of Japan.

On this crag were some strange-looking birds. In noting
them in his record Arellano made the first of his intriguing
observations of the natural history of the area they traversed
on this memorable journey. The birds, wrote Arellano,
were pelicans as big as ostriches. They were, one may
surmise, cormorants outlined at a distance against the sky.

Onward went the *San Lucas*, assisted by winds and currents
from the west. As spring turned to summer, one day was
much like another. Just before they reached the fortieth
parallel a great host of black 'sparrows' flew over the ship
for a day and a night, making an astonishing noise.

Having arrived in latitude 40 degrees north, Lope Martin
pointed out to Arellano the great land of China on his
chart, shown not far north of their position. This indicated
that if they went farther north, they would be in danger of
running on to the coast of China. Therefore, said Lope,
they would run east in forty degrees.

Soon after this the *San Lucas* encountered persistent bad
weather from the south, forcing them northward, while the
sky became so obscured that for many days the sun was not
visible and the pilot was unable to take his position. This
caused them much alarm, since they thought they were in
danger of being driven on the China coast to the north as
shown in the chart.

After many days of these anxieties, there came a time
when the sun showed clear again. The pilot took a sight
on it with his astrolabe and worked out his latitude. He put

a point on the chart to mark their position. This revealed a droll situation indeed. According to the chart they were somewhere in the interior of China.

The early cartographers did not at that time have the advantage of the knowledge gained by experience. Arellano and Lope Martin and the rest of the company of the *San Lucas* were the first Europeans ever to have been in those waters.

By this time the weather was freezingly cold, although it was mid-summer. On 11 June snow fell on the ship and lay on the deck till noon. One of the ship's boys took a bottle of oil to fill the lamps. The oil in it was frozen stiff, and when it had been heated for a while it ran out like flakes of butter.

The fact that the ship's company had lost most of their clothes at Mindanao must have made the cold all the harder to take.

In these high latitudes Arellano made some more zoological notes: 'We saw swimming past us a dog of the sea with feet and hands and tail, and ears, a fox; and later on we saw some more, and one came alongside and began to bark at us, a thing which astonished us all, because nobody had ever seen such creatures: likewise we saw in this ocean fish pigs as big as a cow.' No seals or sea-lions inhabited the waters of Spain.

In going up into these northern latitudes, Lope Martin had taken the *San Lucas* into the zone of westerlies which were to blow Spanish galleons from the Philippines to North America for the following three centuries.

By this time the ship's company were in poor shape. Many of them had developed a curious disease. The flesh of their mouths swelled greatly so that the gums covered the teeth, which fell out when they bit on something hard. This was of course the scurvy.

Another plague which the people of the *San Lucas* encountered was rats. There were at this time five barrels of water left. One day it was found that one of them was empty, and it was at first thought that someone had been at the water. When they examined the barrel more closely, however, they found it had a hole in the bottom where the rats, themselves crazed with thirst, and no doubt detecting a slight seepage through a seam, had gnawed their way through. Still greater was the horror of the sorely tried company when another of the barrels was also found to be holed.

It was decided to mount a guard of four men with a lamp below decks day and night. They chased rats with sticks, killing droves of them.

At the end of June the *San Lucas* began to run out of sails. First they lost the foresail in a storm. They sacrificed one of the bonnets to make a new foresail. The other bonnets were used up in other repairs. The sewing thread ran out, so fishing lines were used.

As July wore on, with storms which forced them down to the 27th parallel, the pilot estimated that the American coast could not be far ahead.

On 18 July, 1565, when dawn was breaking, the people of the *San Lucas* saw the land of North America ahead. It was twelve weeks since they had seen the last sight of the Philippines. The historic first traverse of the Pacific from west to east had been accomplished. Much moved, Arellano gave thanks to God for the mercy he had shown them.

The *San Lucas* had struck the long narrow peninsula of Lower California, as Lope Martin recognized from his chart. These were waters which were known from previous Spanish voyages up the coast from Mexico.

The *San Lucas* ran down the coast of the Lower California

peninsula to its southern point. Here, within a few hundred miles of La Navidad and home, their gravest hour came.

Because of the strength of the wind, before which he was running with the mainsail and foresail, Lope Martin gave orders to shorten the mainsail. While the sailors were aloft gathering in the sail, a sudden blast of wind with heavy cross-seas struck the ship. The wind tore the mainsail from the hands of the seamen and flung two of them to the deck. The ship broached sideways to the waves and heeled over so that a great sea went right through the ship, casting down the helmsman, compass and lamps, and carrying away the spritsail.

The pilot shouted the order to shorten the foresail. The sailors, weakened by thirst, hunger and sickness, groped round in the dark. The mainsail was in ribbons and caught around the stays. As the foresail was taken in, the ship, half-swamped though it was, righted itself.

The only whole sail they now had was the makeshift foresail made previously out of the bonnet. The sailors swore to take it to the House of Our Lady of Guadelupe with an offering if only it held out till they made port. Then the mainsail was patched up with some cloth supplied by the faithful Rivero from his own possessions. Heaven smiled on them again, sending gentle breezes. As they came down the Mexican coast on the last leg of their Odyssey, the blankets from the bunks were used as bonnets to help the *San Lucas* home to La Navidad.

Lope Martin and the company of the *San Lucas* had performed the epic feat of taking the tiny ship some 16,000 miles from America to the Philippines and back, pioneering the way through unknown seas and islands.

4

Friends & Foes

AFTER the *San Lucas* disappeared on 1 December, 1564, in the trackless wastes of the North Pacific, Legazpi's other three ships pressed on to the west. They sailed on for days and weeks. Then, on the morning of 9 January, the watcher in the crow's-nest of the flagship called out 'Land ahead'. This proved to be a small low island divided in two parts by a narrow depression or channel. It was Mejit, the easternmost island of the Marshalls, some 30 miles north of where the *San Lucas* had passed a few days previously.

The ships skirted the north side of the pleasant little palm-covered island, the leadsmen at the prows feeling for bottom without success. They drew round to the west side so close to the land that a man could have leapt from the bowsprit of the flagship onto the reef, so calm was the sea. As they did so a little collection of huts among the palm-trees came in sight, with a beach in front, on which were some people. Two canoes of fishermen were a small distance off shore. When the islanders saw the great ships, appearing suddenly like monstrous visitants, the fishermen fled to the beach, and all the people there ran into the palm groves.

The flagship dropped two anchors in eighty fathoms, but both dragged and the current took the vessel off shore. The *San Pablo* had no better luck. The smaller *San Juan*, however, going so close to the land that its prow bumped against it, got bottom in 140 fathoms. The anchor held, and the ship swung to it close to the shore.

On the flagship Legazpi conferred with his close associates. It was agreed that Martin de Goite, the commander of the company of soldiers on the flagship, should proceed to the island in the pinnace with twenty or thirty of the soldiers as an advance guard. Since Legazpi's instructions from the Real Audiencia in Mexico were that he should remain on board until it was safe to land in strange territory, Legazpi's grandson, Felipe de Salcedo, accompanied by Andres de Urdaneta, the Padre Prior, followed Goite in the ship's boat as Legazpi's emissaries. Felipe was bidden to take possession of the island in the name of King Philip, and Urdaneta went along to see if he could speak to the islanders and make the Spanish intentions known to them.

Mateo del Saz, the captain of the *San Pablo*, and Juan de la Isla, the captain of the *San Juan*, who had put off in their ships' boats for the flagship, joined the little flotilla on its way to the beach.

When the landing-party was on shore, they moved up the beach towards the huts. All the people had taken refuge in the palms with the exception of an old man and woman, and a younger woman with a baby.

Urdaneta addressed to the old man a few words learned by him at Guam in 1526. The old man and the women showed no sign of comprehension. The friar held out some beads and trinkets as an offering of friendship. The old man hesitated and then took the curious ornaments from him. The women, likewise overcome with curiosity, took some of them also. When Urdaneta offered the old woman a mirror, her astonishment and delight were great, and acceptance of Urdaneta and his companions was thus assured.

The old man now beckoned to the visitors to come to his hut, where fish and many coconuts were stored, and gave some of these to them.

By this time the other islanders, who had been peering

at the strangers from the groves round about, began to come out. The people were good-looking, with smooth hair down to their waists. The men were naked apart from some fine beards, for which reason the island was called Los Barbudos – the Bearded Ones. The women wore palm petticoats. No weapons were seen all the time the Spaniards were at the island. The visitors were much charmed with the picture of simple contentment, peace and plenty it exhibited. There were little gardens in which yams and other roots were grown. Fowls wandered at will. The coconut groves provided food and drink. Fish were caught in plenty both with nets and with bone hooks on long lines, the hooks being cunningly made from two separate pieces of bone bound together at an angle. The whole island was only a few miles round, and there seemed to be no more than a hundred people on it.

The startling contrast between the unwarlike character of the islanders of Mejit and those of other islands was no doubt due to the fact that Mejit was well away from the other inhabited islands and was not therefore continually menaced by attacks.

Felipe and the scribe, Hernan Riquel, were now in a position to testify that the islanders had offered no resistance to the acts of possession taken by the Europeans. Felipe cut a few branches of trees and gathered some vegetation from the ground in token of occupation, and then claimed the island for the King of Spain. All this Riquel solemnly recorded in a document which in due course found its way into the Spanish archives, whereupon the islanders of Mejit, and the Kings of Spain, ignored one another for several centuries.

The sinking of the sun, coupled with a gun from the flagship, told Urdaneta and the captains that it was time to go.

When the villagers saw them prepare to leave, they were moved to open sorrow, as were the Spaniards themselves.

Some delay was caused because the pinnace had been left on dry land by the receding tide, and the islanders helped the soldiers and sailors to manhandle it into the surf. It was 10 o'clock before the party regained the ships and the journey was resumed.

After leaving Mejit the ships traversed the Marshalls, passing close by the atolls of Ailuk, Jemo, Wotho and Ujelang without finding bottom for anchorage and without seeing any signs of human habitation.

So unknown were the seas and immense the distances that the pilots had only the vaguest notion where they were. They argued that they could not be far from the Philippines. Urdaneta, however, considered that they were still well short of the meridian of Guam, and stoutly maintained his opinion in the face of the smiling unbelief of the pilots. Since Guam was in the 13th parallel of latitude, it was agreed that it would do no harm to bear north-west into that parallel and then follow it to the west.

Thirteen days after leaving Mejit, a high, fine-looking island came into sight, its volcanic peaks showing red in the sun above the green forest below. It turned out to be Guam, the southernmost and largest of the Marianas. Urdaneta thus had the laugh over the pilots.

As the ships drew round to the south-west coast of Guam in the lee of the island from the prevailing north-east wind, hundreds of canoes came out to meet them, astonishing the sailors with their swiftness and grace. Many Europeans who visited Guam in later times were similarly to record their enchantment with the Marianas craft. By judging the force of the wind as it blew over the outrigger into the sail, the sailing-master could keep his vessel trimmed with the outrigger float just skimming the water for 200 yards or more at a time, making the canoe run like a skate on a blade. The sail was the triangular lateen, with the forefoot fastened to the bow. The outrigger had always to be kept on the windward side, and when changing on to the other tack some of the crew would quickly bring the forefoot of the sail from the one end of the canoe to the other, fastening it to the former stern, which then became the bow. The mast, which was slanting, was slewed round in its socket so as to slope back again when the vessel had changed to the other tack. All this was done in less than a minute, and the vessel would skim off again on the other tack.

At midnight the *San Juan* got bottom and dropped her anchor in a bay at the south-west side of Guam. The two big ships stood off till dawn, and then anchored alongside the *San Juan*.

Guam is a fair-sized island about thirty miles long from north to south. Fertile and populous, it has since its discovery by Magellan played a leading part in the comings and goings of a long succession of Spanish, Dutch, British, French, Russian, German, Japanese and American ships.

The morning after Legazpi's ships reached Guam, a notice was posted and read out loud, saying that the islanders must be treated well, and that all trade must be done through the Crown officials. No sooner was the sun up than canoes from the shore began to arrive at the ships with goods to trade, until more than four hundred craft could be counted. They offered coconuts, both dry and green, sugarcane, fresh plantains, and rice cakes. For these the Spaniards traded scissors, mirrors, bits of iron, linen, beads and other trinkets.

Urdaneta, being probably the only European then living who had visited Guam before, said a few words to the people in one of the canoes in the Chamorro tongue of the Marianas, at which all those in earshot chattered in pleased surprise.

One old man in one of the canoes called out 'Gonzalo, Gonzalo'.

Urdaneta explained to the other Spaniards who were watching that the reference was to Gonzalo de Vigo, a Spaniard who had deserted in the Marianas in 1523 from the *Trinidad* when it was trying to get back to Mexico after Magellan's death. When, in 1526, the *Santa Maria de la Victoria*, with Urdaneta on board, had arrived at Guam, the ship's company had been amazed to find themselves hailed from one of the canoes by a Spaniard, who in due course explained how he had deserted from the *Trinidad*. Vigo was taken away in the *Santa Maria de la Victoria* and later got a pardon.

The people of Guam were adjudged a fine-looking lot. The men were strong and handsome, with long straight hair caught in the nape of the neck. As in the other islands the only clothing of any consequence was the palm petticoat worn by the women.

The business of trading with the canoes that came out to the ships now reached major dimensions. The payment preferable to the islanders was iron, which they coveted for making their canoes instead of coconut fibre. Nails and spikes were thus the main medium of exchange. By order of the Real Audiencia of Mexico the trading was supervised by the three Crown officials, Guido de la Bezares the treasurer, Andres de la Cauchela the accountant, and Andres de Mirandaola the factor. The purpose of this supervision was so that the price of the official purchases should not be forced up, and so that the fifth part due to the Crown from any gold or precious metal that was bought from the islanders should be levied. But no gold or silver was forthcoming from Guam.

After a time the officials began to find that the people of Guam knew a thing or two about the tricks of the grocery trade. The canoemen delivered their goods by fastening them to ropes for hauling up to the ships' decks after payment in

nails or other goods had been sent down to them by the
same means. Now and again the attention of an official
would be called to a load of yams or bananas or rice which
was sent up from a canoe, and which proved on inspection to
contain about two fingers' depth of food on top and sand or
grass or stones below. Another deception consisted of
supplying coconut oil mixed with water so that the oil
floated on top covering the water below. Nor did the traders
always await payment by orthodox means, being not above
pulling out the spikes from the sides of the ships if a close
watch were not kept on them.

A cheerful irresponsibility was shown by many of the
visitors to the ships, as by one who tried to get away with a
ship's boat which had been tied at the side of one of the
ships. When he was observed from the deck a stentorian
shout from the sailors caused him to make off in his canoe,
when he laughed heartily at his own discomfiture. On
another occasion the visitors in one canoe made persistent
signs to one sailor to get into their vessel, and when he did
so to show that a proud Spanish sailor was not afraid of them,
they made off for the shore so fast that discretion triumphed
over pride and the sailor jumped into the water and swam
back to the ship.

All these indignities the Spaniards suffered without taking
reprisals, for such were Legazpi's orders.

On the third day at Guam the Captains Mateo del Saz and
Martin de Goite and Juan de la Isla proceeded at the request
of Legazpi in the ships' boats to the head of the bay in which
the ships were anchored in order to see if there was fresh
water there, as the ships' casks were in need of replenishing.
They found that there was an estuary leading to a river of fine
sweet water. The next day the ships came close to the entrance of the estuary.

The *San Juan*, being a small ship, was deputed to go on a reconnaissance up the estuary and into the river. As the ship drew into the river, an engaging scene met the eyes of Juan de la Isla and his crew. Ahead of them was a large collection of houses in the palm groves on the bank of the river. Behind the settlement the forested slopes rose steeply, making a picturesque tropic scene.

Their attention then became concentrated on something less agreeable. A number of warriors were gathered together a short distance ahead of the ship on the river bank. In front of them they had thrust their spears into the ground so as to leave their hands free to manipulate their slings. At their feet they had palm baskets full of sling-stones in the shape of eggs.

As the ship came slowly in range, a hail of stones descended on the decks of the *San Juan*. Whereas on the open sea the sailors could take cover, in these narrow waters the management of the vessel required that they stand to their posts.

The captain ordered Aragozes, the quartermaster, to get out the arquebuses. By this time the attackers, who were shouting and much excited, were coming into the shallows in order to get a closer aim at the crew on the ship. A stone from a sling struck Isla himself on the head. The first volley from the muskets, however, stopped the attackers in their tracks, and they turned and fled.

When the *San Juan* rejoined the other ships, and the hostility of the defenders of the settlement was reported, Legazpi asked Saz to go with a party of soldiers in a ship's boat and try to make the people understand that all that they wanted was water, and that they intended no harm to the settlement.

Saz accordingly went with a boatload of men and managed to pacify the people at the river mouth by indicating to them that all that was wanted was water. The *San Juan* anchored near the mouth of the river without further molestation.

The next day the ships' boats began plying back and forth to the river, filling the casks with water. For a time all was peace and friendship with the people on shore, who helped the landing-parties to fill the casks and put them in the boats.

Suddenly there was a great hubbub, and a man was seen running off with an arquebus which he had snatched from one of the soldiers, whereupon numbers of the other warriors took off after him in frightened flight. They took cover in the trees on the slope beyond the river flat, and started to fling stones down on the landing-party which was ashore at the time.

This was too much for Captain Saz, who ordered his soldiers to pepper the thief and his companions with small shot. Immediately they made overtures for peace, and Saz suffered them to come back, without, however, recovering the musket.

The work went forward uneasily in this way for a time, when another incident happened. This time an islander, having been either offended or in some way frightened by one of the soldiers, struck the man in the chest with a spear. The soldier's breastplate deflected the blow, but he received a wound in the hand which became infected, causing his death ten or twelve days later.

As before, the assailant and his companions rushed off up the slopes, took cover, and began to hurl stones with their slings. The Spaniards this time pursued the attack. One of the warriors was captured and taken in shackles to the ship, the people of the settlement being told that he would be held as a hostage until the stolen musket had been returned. Later, however, the prisoner jumped overboard and escaped, taking his shackles with him.

c

Once more peace was restored, and the time was judged ripe for the ceremony of taking possession of Guam. Legazpi for the first time came ashore, the pacification of the island being regarded as sufficiently achieved. With him went the six monks headed by Urdaneta, to celebrate Mass.

Numbers of soldiers formed a backdrop to the impressive scene, while upwards of eighty islanders gathered curiously around. To the latter Legazpi ordered that beads and other gifts be given in token of peace and friendship.

Here is the graphic description of the occasion by the scribe Hernan Riquel: 'On the 26th day of the month of January of the year 1565, being at one of the Ladrones which the inhabitants gave to understand by signs was called Guam, the very illustrious lord Miguel Lopez de Legazpi, Governor and Captain-General for His Majesty of the company and Armada which goes in his Royal service to discover the Isles of the West, having disembarked at the inlet where he made his watering-place, before me, Hernan Riquel, Chief Scribe of the said Isles of the West, said that in the name of His Royal Majesty Don Philip our Lord and as his Governor and Captain-General, he was taking and did take occupancy and possession officially and effectively of the said island and others contiguous and subject thereto, and in token of authentic possession took his sword and cut branches of trees and cleared away herbage and cast aside rocks and caused some crosses to be placed on trees, to wit some coconut palms which are close to the shore, and caused Masses to be said and celebrated by the ecclesiastics of the Order of Saint Augustine who go in the said fleet.'

This claim was in due course made good, for Guam became a staging-post for Spanish ships and centre of Spanish dominion in the Marianas for several centuries.

In the days that followed Legazpi's first landing on Guam, the settlement near the watering-place became familiar to the visitors.

Near the watering-place at the mouth of the river was a very large community house. It was put there because one of its purposes was to house some very large and valuable canoes. It was so spacious that it could hold 200 people in addition to the canoes. Here Mass was celebrated each day by the monks during the time that the ships were anchored nearby.

Farther on were the houses of the village, scattered through the palms in picturesque fashion. They were remarkably well made, considering that the people had only stone adzes to work with. They were raised well clear of the ground on pillars made of stone blocks, and were made of logs covered with palm leaves or matting tied with coconut fibre, and had attractive windows. From a central hall sleeping rooms opened out on each side. Separate small low huts were used as kitchens. Near the settlement were pleasant cultivations, while round about were plantain trees as well as the ubiquitous coconut palms. At the back of the little town the forest ran up the slopes to the steep bare peaks above.

There were many little settlements like this all along the west side of the island, as the chief pilot, Esteban Rodriguez, found when he went on a tour of exploration in the pinnace. There were three or four fine bays with good anchorage, and rivers of sweet water flowing into them. At each of the villages the people resisted the Spaniards with stones flung from their slings, but the landing-parties, being armed with bucklers, breastplates and arquebuses, drove them off with some loss of life.

Now had the ships gone off after a week at Guam with their supplies of food and water replenished, both the visitors and the islanders would have parted reasonably well pleased with one another. But it was not to be.

On the first day of February, 1565, after the expedition

had been at Guam for a week, the ships' boats were plying
back and forth to the watering-place fetching water. Martin
de Goite, the captain in charge of the soldiers on the flagship,
told his cabin-boy to go ashore with the boat and stretch his
legs. The lad, who was much liked both by the soldiers and
the crew, went in with the flagship's boat on its next trip.
After landing the lad strolled round for a while, watching the
scene as the men, helped by some of the local people, filled
the casks, while a few soldiers mounted guard. The people
of Guam were, as usual, very cheerful, and danger seemed
far away.

After a while the boy, feeling drowsy in the afternoon
heat, went off to the palm grove nearby, and lay down in the
shade, his thoughts perhaps idly turning to his home and
loved ones far away in Spain. Soon he was fast asleep.

The sun was setting, the last loads of water were put into
the boats, and the crewmen and soldiers climbed aboard.
The boat of the flagship arrived at the ship's side, the casks
were hoisted on deck, and the boat's party came aboard.

Suddenly a great noise of excited yelling came across the
water from the watering-place. The sailors asked themselves
what it was all about. Their wonderment turned to alarm
when they realized the cabin-boy was missing.

With fear and anguish lending strength to their strokes,
the boat's crew were in an instant back in the boat and
rowing furiously to the land. As they drew near, they saw
that their worst fears were confirmed. In the sand at the
edge of the water the lifeless body of the lad lay where it had
been transfixed by the shouting islanders with their lances.
When the assassins saw the ship's boat, they left the beach
and ran off to the slope of the hill at a distance.

When the sailors reached the body, a grim sight met their
pitying gaze. The boy was spread-eagled naked, his hands
tied with coconut cord. In the body some thirty lance

wounds were counted, as well as many bruises from blows by stones. As a final indignity a sharp stake had been thrust through the mouth.

While the crewmen took up the body with mounting indignation and conveyed it to the flagship, the warriors on the hill jeered fiercely at them, waving the boy's shirt, breeches and jacket in provocative disdain.

All the time that this horrid diversion was going on, the canoemen who were trading with the ships continued their business as if nothing untoward was happening. The people of Guam and the nearby islands were constantly at war with one another. Dwelling in the shadow of violence and death, they had learnt to live with these ever-present threats.

When the people on the ships saw the boy's body on the deck of the flagship, cold fury rose in their hearts. Many a man is moved to kill when he sees the lifeless body of his friend. The captains and officials all agreed that this was indeed a legitimate cause for war.

Straightway that night Mateo del Saz assumed his role of military commander. He gathered a hundred soldiers who, armed and accoutred, were taken by the pinnace and the ships' boats to the shore. As soon as dawn broke they bore down on the settlement.

How different things were now from the cheerful, chattering, animated scene which had greeted the visitors a few days before. Not a soul was in the settlement. Only the household goods of the people, and the large canoes, remained. The inhabitants had put into practice their ancient strategy of total withdrawal.

Captain Saz selected a squad of twenty men and gave orders to their leader. They were to take cover in the palms near the watering-place, while the main party set fire to the canoes and then embarked. It was hoped that by this artifice the local people might come out from hiding when they saw the boats go, whereupon the ambushers were to let them have a volley and feel their steel.

The trap was laid stealthily, the chosen men going into the palms by a roundabout route one or two at a time. Then the main party put torches to the canoes, quickly got into the boats, and pushed off.

When the boats were some distance from the shore, a number of the local warriors, who had evidently been hiding on the forested slopes nearby, came down to the shore. Some of them started to scoop up water to put out the fires on the canoes.

The platoon commander gave the command to fire. The arquebuses roared, and three of the warriors at the shore edge fell wounded. All the rest, with a celerity acquired from long experience in the sudden attack and the sudden retreat, fled to the slopes. All, that is, except one. As the soldiers ran in their heavy accoutrements like tortoises after hares, this man fell, and was seized by the vanguard of the soldiers.

Back to the beach now came Saz with the boats. Looking at the three mortally wounded men on the ground, and the cowering captive, he was much disappointed that this was all the vengeance that had been granted. He ordered the three wounded men to be hanged on the trees by the place where the cabin-boy had been murdered, telling the executioners to do this quickly before the victims cheated justice by dying. The men, already moribund, were soon corpses swinging on branches of trees in the palm grove.

Saz now gave the order to hang the terrified captive. While the executions had been going on, some of the monks had come in a ship's boat. The monks intervened with Saz for the prisoner's life, saying that it would be more fitting to God and the service of His Majesty to take the man to New Spain where the friars could learn his language and so prepare the way for those of the Order of St Augustine who would come to Guam later as missionaries. Saz agreed to this request, and the captive was taken by the monks on board one of the ships.

The time had now come to press on to the west. On 3 February the ships sailed from Guam for the Philippines. Ten days later, on 13 February, 1565, the high land of Samar came in sight. Legazpi had at last arrived in the Isles of the West.

5

Hide-&-Seek in the
Philippines

WHEN Legazpi's three ships came in sight of Samar on
13 February, 1565, the *San Lucas* was lying in Davao Gulf in
Mindanao, some hundreds of miles to the south. This wide
separation resulted from the decision of Legazpi, at Urdaneta's
urging, to make a change of course from the tenth parallel
of latitude to the thirteenth in order to make Guam,
following on which Legazpi's ships continued on to the
Philippines in higher latitudes than had the *San Lucas*.

Having thus arrived on the east coast of Samar, the three
ships anchored in the lee of some small islands near the shore.

The expedition's primary need was for a good port with a
safe anchorage, with plenty of food available in the vicinity.
Before the finding of such a haven was achieved, many
strange encounters were to befall the visitors from across
the sea.

On the day after their arrival, three ships' boats, with
eighty men, traversed the Samar coast near the anchorage.
For a time it seemed that there were no habitations, for the
foreshore and the entrances to the streams which flowed into
the bay were masked by mangroves and palms. But after a
time the boats came to a spot where a number of huts could
be seen near a beach, on which some fifty of the local people
were gathered. The Spaniards found that they could not

speak with them except by signs, and had to content themselves with making some small gifts as a sign of friendship.

The following day a canoe came off to the ships, and Legazpi sent down to the people in it some beads and scarlet bonnets and knives. This had the desired effect, for in the following days numbers of canoes came to the anchorage, some of them bringing local Samar chiefs.

There were on board the flagship two men who knew something of the East Indian languages. One was the Padre Prior, Urdaneta himself, who had picked up quite a deal of the Moluccan and Malay tongues during his sojourn of nine years in the East Indies thirty to forty years previously. There was also an official interpreter, Geronimo Pacheco, who gained fluency in Malay during a previous residence in the Portuguese possessions on the Strait of Malacca. But neither Urdaneta nor Pacheco could understand the Filipinos, nor make themselves understood.

The Spaniards now had an opportunity of seeing at close quarters their intended subjects. Esteban Rodriguez, the chief pilot, made some invaluable notes of what he saw, as the Samar chiefs and their followers came and went in these first few days. Gold pendants hung from their ears, and the chiefs wore gold anklets also. The only clothing worn by most of the men was a piece of cloth covering the loins. Their entire torsos, thighs and arms were tattooed with pigment deep in the flesh, the extent of the tattooing being regarded as a mark of their bravery, as indeed it was. The warriors carried small lances with large iron heads, and daggers of well-wrought design. Some of them had bows and arrows, but the bows had little tension and the arrows were without feathers. The most intriguing custom, however, was that of sealing a friendship by the drinking of blood and wine. Each of the two or three persons who joined in this ceremony drew some drops of blood from his chest or arm with the

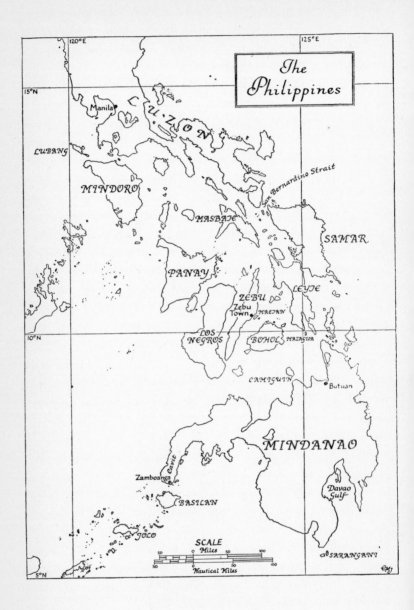

The Philippines

tip of a dagger so that the blood was delivered into a vessel containing wine, which was then drunk by the participants.

One day a huge canoe, carved from prow to stern, and rowed by thirty paddlers, came to the ship. Thirty men came on board, bearing copper instruments which they beat as drums.

The local people traded small amounts of palm wine, rice, plantains, fowls and pigs for Spanish hats, beads, pearls, mirrors and scissors, but nothing remotely adequate in the way of food could be got out of them. Furthermore there was no safe port anywhere close at hand. Some of the visiting chiefs, however, said that there was a good port on the Samar coast farther north, or so it was understood from their signs. Legazpi therefore decided to send Captain Juan de la Isla with a small company in one of the ship's boats to see what he could find in that direction.

A few days later the boat returned. Even before Juan de la Isla spoke, it was plain from his mien that things had not gone well. Isla reported that they had gone in the boat more than twenty miles, and found only two bays, but no place where the ships could be safe. Nor could they think well of the people there, for Don Francisco Gomez, one of Legazpi's retinue of gentlemen, had been done to death before the eyes of his companions.

Isla then recounted the sad story of Gomez's death. At a bay to the north, some of the local Samar people came down to the shore and made signs of peace to the boat. The chief presented a dagger to his own chest as an invitation to the Spanish leader to drink blood and wine as a seal on their friendship. So Gomez, saying he would take up the chief's offer, and without awaiting word from Isla, impetuously leapt ashore and began to go through the blood ceremony with the chief. But even as he was doing this, a man came out of a nearby thicket and, ranging alongside Gomez, thrust a lance into his ribs so that he fell and expired at once. The boat's company landed as swiftly as possible, but by the time they reached Gomez, the assassin and his companions had disappeared.

This incident obviously became known also in the villages near the ships, for thereafter no more people came out to the anchorage or were seen on shore, no doubt for fear that vengeance might be wreaked on them.

The lack of a port and of food supplies, coupled with the discouraging reactions of the local inhabitants, made Legazpi and his officers decide to follow the Samar coast to the south.

After two days' sailing down the coast, the ships anchored in a large bay. Near the anchorage, among the mangroves fringing the shore, was the village of Cuniungo. Here friendly relations were established with two chiefs who promised to supply rice and pigs and fowls, but with that fickleness which the Spaniards were coming to expect, the chiefs neither sent food nor came back to the ships.

It was now decided that Captain Martin de Goite should lead an exploratory party to the south. The pinnace and one of the ship's boats were supplied with guns and food, and the pilots Esteban Rodriguez and Rodrigo de la Isla, with fifty men, were sent with Goite. Their instructions were to return within ten days.

Legazpi and his associates now found themselves with time on their hands as they waited for Goite's return. They accordingly decided to see if they could make friends with the people of the nearby village. They were in need of food, and Legazpi was loth to give up hope of conciliating the islanders. This sentiment was fully endorsed by the monks, whose mission it was to propagate the Christian faith in the islands. The soldiers were inclined to be a little more cavalier in their dealings with the people.

Full of hope, Legazpi and the monks, together with Captain Saz, embarked for the shore in the ships' boats with a number of sailors and soldiers. As they worked their way through the mangroves towards Cuniungo, they heard much shouting.

When the boats had traversed the mangroves and the village came in sight, the hostile character of the reception awaiting them was only too obvious. On the beach the village warriors, brandishing their weapons and shouting threateningly, were excitedly pacing back and forth.

When the visitors held up some trinkets in sight of the concourse on shore in token of friendship, so far from pacifying them, this evoked violent gesticulations. Some of the swordsmen, carried away with the ardour of war, hacked at the shrubs near the shore in symbolic representation of what would happen to anybody who dared to land.

Legazpi felt himself in a dilemma as between giving the appearance of cowardice in the sight of the islanders, or turning what had been intended to be a visit of goodwill into a punitive one. He showed that he was a man of no small mind by ordering the boats to withdraw. This, however, was no easy task, for immediately the warriors, thinking they had the enemy on the run, started to throw stones at the Spaniards and follow up their advantage in their canoes.

There was a limit to Legazpi's forbearance in suffering this danger to his people, and as the sling-stones rained on the boats, he gave the order to fire two muskets to frighten off the assailants.

The shots had the usual dramatically discouraging effect. The sudden noise, and the sight and feel of the small shot falling in and around the leading canoes, caused them to stop dead and then make for the shore in confusion.

At the end of ten days Captain Goite returned with the

pinnace and ship's boat from his quest along the Samar coast
to the south. He had come to Leyte Gulf, and had crossed it
to the east coast of Leyte. Here another tragedy had taken
place, when a serving-lad, having strayed away from a
landing-party, had been ambushed. A lance thrown at him
from the ambush wounded him, and he died within three
days. Farther down the coast of Leyte they came to a large
settlement named Cabalian, with many cultivations and
much livestock, but no port. Goite then returned so as to be
back to the ships within the allowed ten days.

The Armada now followed Goite's track to Cabalian,
near the south-eastern extremity of Leyte, hoping at least to
get food there, since supplies by this time were very short.
As the ships came to anchor, Legazpi and his officers on the
flagship gazed approvingly toward the shore.

The settlement of Cabalian numbered many houses in
prolific palm groves. Pigs, fowls and dogs could be seen
wandering round among the trees and huts. Behind the
settlement rose a range of hills, on the slopes of which could
be seen many more houses and groves, with fields of rice
and other crops.

A boat was sent ashore with instructions to indicate to the
chief of the settlement that Legazpi desired to seal a bond of
friendship with blood and wine, and to ask the chief to come
on board for this purpose. Soon a canoe came off with a
young chief and two or three followers. He managed to
convey that his name was Camutuan, that he was the son of
the main chief of Cabalian, that his father was an old man,
and that he himself would confirm peaceful relations with
blood and wine.

The ceremonious Spaniards had a consultation among
themselves on this difficult question of protocol. It was
considered that Legazpi himself could deal only with the
head chief. It was accordingly decided that the ensign, Andres

de Ibarra, who was of an age with the young chief, should
represent Legazpi for the purpose of drinking blood and wine.

Ibarra concerted with the chief's son in the ceremony,
which was performed with due attention to its barbaric
detail. Camutuan then gave the young ensign the chiefly
headgear he was wearing, and the ensign returned the com-
pliment with a gift of cloth. Legazpi followed this up by
giving all the visitors an assortment of beads, mirrors,
scarlet hats and the like, and showed them that he would
give them as much as they wanted of such trade goods in
return for pigs, fowls and rice. The dusky envoys assured him
that these would be brought the next day, and then went
ashore.

That evening Legazpi felt that at last he had reason to
think that his diplomacy was paying off.

Later that night Legazpi and his officers were called to the
deck by the watch. They saw that on shore the people of the
settlement were embarking their women and children and
gear in numbers of canoes and sending them along the coast.
The villagers were working with concentrated energy on an
evacuation of their property and dependants.

Legazpi decided that if he tried to stop them there would
only be trouble, and hoped that by leaving them alone they
might still be persuaded to come to him.

The next day, however, no canoes came out to the ship.
Geronimo Pacheco was therefore bidden to shout out in
Malay to the shore that no harm would come to the people,
and that they would be well paid for food. These appeals were
interspersed with words in the local Philippine tongue
which the Spaniards were now getting to know. Once, twice
and thrice these appeals were delivered from the flagship's
deck. Some of the men on shore were seen to come and
listen, as if they understood. But still no canoes were
launched, either with or without food.

Legazpi now called the ensign Ibarra. He asked him to make contact with the people on shore, the thought being that they might take notice of Ibarra since he had drunk blood and wine with their young chief the previous day.

When Ibarra and his party neared the shore, they were pleased to find that the young chief Camutuan himself was there, and that he accepted their invitation to come out again to the flagship. Camutuan, when he met Legazpi again, gave him to understand that his people were in great fear of the huge ships, and that his father, the head chief, was too old and blind to come. Camutuan agreed to send some of his companions ashore to try to persuade the villagers to bring food to the ships, but all that happened when these envoys went in to land was that a few more men came out and joined Camutuan on the ship. Camutuan and his followers were themselves very content to remain on the ship.

Legazpi now summoned a conference of his captains and the Crown officials, and suggested to them that they had no recourse but to send a landing-party ashore and take food forcibly, paying for it in trade goods.

This was agreed to be essential, and Goite was deputed to take a party ashore, with the Crown officials in attendance to supervise the trading.

As the boats went in to shore, the men were told not to fire on the villagers or provoke them in any way, and to show everything they got to the officials so that it could be paid for.

When the boats reached land, however, all the villagers of Cabalian immediately fled to the hills, leaving Goite and his men in possession of the settlement and its yams and live-stock.

That day the landing-party managed to find and convey to the ships 45 pigs and 30 loads of root crop. They did not have much luck with the fowls, because these were quick on the wing and kept eluding capture.

Solemnly the officials decided what was fair payment in beads, scarlet bonnets, knives, scissors and the like, and placed them before Camutuan to send ashore to his people. Camutuan deputed one of his followers to take them ashore, and off this man went in a canoe.

Before long, however, there were shouts from the shore, on which a number of villagers had gathered. Legazpi sent a boat in to find out what they wanted. When the boat got back the crew reported that the people on shore had rounded up a fine pig that had eluded the foragers, and were offering it as a ransom for the return of Camutuan himself.

Legazpi sent back a message that Camutuan and his companions stayed on board by their own wish, and could leave any time they liked.

Camutuan and his three companions on the flagship were now perfectly at ease, and great strides were made in understanding their words. The young Filipinos explained to their hosts the geography of the islands to the south. The peaks of Mindanao could be seen in the distance. Between Cabalian and Mindanao were the small islands of Mazagua and Camiguin, as Camutuan explained.

The name Mazagua – the modern Limasawa – meant something to the Spaniards, because the people of this island had shown friendship to one of the vessels of Villalobos's expedition when it had visited them more than twenty years previously. It was now decided to go there, and Camutuan and his companions agreed to go along with them to show them the way.

The Armada came down to Mazagua, close to the south-eastern point of Leyte. On the way there Legazpi had a suit of blue velvet and a scarlet mantle with blue velvet panels made as an intended present for the chief of Mazagua.

When Mazagua came in sight, the Armada hove to and Urdaneta and Saz went ahead as envoys in the ships' boats. On the way Urdaneta explained to Saz, as they approached the eastern coast of Mazagua, that the accounts of Villalobos's expedition showed that there was a thriving village at the island, where the chief and his people had proved very friendly, and that there was a good port beyond the village.

As the boats drew near the supposed site of the village, however, only an odd hut or two could be seen, with no sign of any inhabitants. The Spaniards went on to the west side of the island, seeing no people on the way. Here a solitary man was seen on a high pinnacle of rock. When he saw them he called out to them inquiringly, as if to ask who they were and why they came. The Spaniards shouted out that they were Castellanos – Spaniards of Castile.

The sound of this name had an electrifying effect on the man on the rock. He immediately clambered down a cord ladder which gave access to and from his eyrie on the rock. Instead of coming down to the beach, however, the man ran swiftly to his hut nearby, disappeared inside for a while, and then came out and ran back to his rock. As he did so it was seen that he had set fire to his hut which was in flames. The man climbed back to the security of his eagle's nest, removed his ladder, and yelled defiance at the boats.

Sorrowfully Urdaneta and Saz took the boats back to the ships, where another conference was held. It was suspected that something had happened to make the local people afraid of European visitors. But why in that case had the man on the rock appeared friendly until he heard the name of Spain, since no Spanish ships had been in the area for over twenty years?

Legazpi's attention was now directed to Camiguin, an island to the south-west of Mazagua. Here, according to

Camutuan, there was much spice. It was decided to go to it in the hope of finding the shelter and supplies they needed.

The time had now come for Camutuan and his companions to return to Cabalian. Some biscuits and pork and a jar of water were put in their canoe, and Legazpi and the young chief took leave of one another regretfully. The Filipinos had been attired by their hosts in green jackets and breeches and Castilian hats. They moved swiftly away in the canoe, joining together two fingers of their hands towards the flagship in token of friendship and farewell.

Camutuan took with him from Legazpi a letter addressed to Captain Arellano of the *San Lucas*, in case the missing ship should show up in Leyte Gulf. At this time, in actual fact, the *San Lucas* was coming round the south and west side of Mindanao. The gap between the lost ship and the Armada was closing, although neither party knew it.

At Camiguin the Spaniards had no more luck than at Mazagua. They saw a few islanders at one place, but these fled to the interior on the approach of the visitors. A landing-party visited some huts which could be seen from the sea, but again the owners had deserted them, leaving their pigs and fowls in their haste to avoid the invaders of their domain.

It was therefore decided to go the short distance which separated Camiguin from the north coast of Mindanao, which could be seen from Camiguin. But contrary winds drove the ships back, so that they found themselves close to the large island of Bohol. Here they took refuge in a good port in an inlet on the south-west part of Bohol.

The *San Juan* was sent on an exploratory trip to Mindanao, and in the meantime while awaiting its return, repairs were begun on the two big ships in the inlet at Bohol.

In the Bohol inlet the *San Pablo*, under the command of Captain Saz, was nearer the mouth of the inlet than the flagship *San Pedro*, and could look out thence to the open sea.

The day after the arrival, Captain Saz was surprised to hear the lookout call that a strange ship was in sight to the west of Bohol.

A three-masted sailing ship of about the size of the *San Lucas*, but certainly not that vessel, was in the offing. Saz immediately ordered out the boat, and sent five soldiers with the boat's crew to investigate the stranger.

After the boat had gone off, Saz went to the flagship to report. Legazpi was uneasy at the smallness of the force that had gone to the strange vessel, and therefore instructed Saz and Goite to go in the flagship's boat with as many soldiers as it would take, in case there was trouble.

Meanwhile the people in the boat from the *San Pablo* had come near the strange ship. It was being expertly handled and was rigged in European fashion, and yet there did not seem to be any Europeans aboard. Furthermore the ship's company, although brown men, were unlike the Filipinos in that they wore more clothes.

The soldiers and sailors in the boat now made signs to the people on the ship to follow them into the inlet. Instead of doing so, however, a culverin and two muskets were fired from the ship at the Spaniards, and these shots were followed up by a shower of iron-headed arrows and lances. A lance hit one of the sailors, one Diego Hernandez, in the throat, mortally wounding him.

By this time the flagship's boat, with Saz, Goite and a full complement of soldiers, coming under sail with a following wind, had joined the advance party. In vain did Saz make gestures of peace towards the strangers. They kept on firing, and since their vessel was much higher out of the water than the two ships' boats, the people in the latter were under heavy punishment.

Saz now ordered his arquebusiers to return the fire.

Since there were more than a score of experienced musketeers with protective corselets and helmets in the boats, they
soon began to have the advantage over the strangers. As the
action went on, many of the Spaniards were wounded,
particularly by small, well-made arrows which occasionally
penetrated between the meshes of their chain-mail. But
steady toll was taken of the people on board the ship by the
fusillades of the arquebuses, including both scatter-shot and
ball. Finally, as the Spaniards afterwards learnt, the captain
of the ship was killed outright. Some of the survivors then
abandoned ship in a canoe which was at the stern, and made
their escape to another island. The rest, numbering seven,
surrendered on the vessel. Of the ship's company, numbering
45 men before the engagement, fifteen were dead on the
decks when the Spaniards boarded the ship, which was thus
subjugated. Saz then sent ahead his wounded, numbering
twenty men, in one of the boats. With the other boat he took
the ship in tow, and brought it into the inlet to the galleons.

The seven captives were in due course assembled on the
deck of the *San Pedro*. It was found that two of them could
speak Malay, and Urdaneta and Pacheco were able to con-
verse with them.

One of the spokesmen explained that the vessel was from
Borneo, being owned by a Portuguese resident there. They
had come to the Philippines with goods belonging to the
King of Borneo, in order to trade. The spokesman himself
was the pilot, and his Malay-speaking friend was the King's
agent. They belonged to the Moslem faith.

When the Borneo pilot was asked why the Spanish boats
had been attacked when making overtures of friendship, he
answered that their peaceful intentions had not been understood, and the ship's company had thought they had to defend
themselves.

When these facts were conveyed to Legazpi, he told the

strangers that the whole affair had been a grievous misunderstanding, and that the King of Spain desired to be
friendly with everybody in the Indies, including the King and
people of Borneo. He ordered the prisoners to be freed
forthwith, and to be treated as guests for as long as they cared
to stay, whereupon the ship and its contents would be
returned to them. When it was found that many of the goods
on the ship had been seized by the sailors and soldiers as
prizes of war, Legazpi insisted that every last item be dis-
gorged and returned, much to the chagrin of the temporary
owners.

The Borneo pilot, whose name was Tuasan, turned out to be
a much-informed and intelligent man. He was fluent in the
Philippines tongues as well as Malay, and knew all the gossip
of the islands. He was a 'Moro', as the Spaniards called the
Mohammedans, after the Moors who had been their ad-
versaries for centuries previously. No love was lost between
the Christian Spaniards and the followers of the Moslem
faith. As for the 'Moros' of the East Indies, most of them
were native people of those islands who had been converted
to the Moslem faith by invaders from Malaya and India. But
Legazpi's instructions were to try to establish friendly
relations with all the peoples in the Isles of the West,
whatever their religion or cultural background.

The goods on the Borneo ship, and the information given
by Tuasan, give a fascinating glimpse of the trade of the
Indies at this time. The main source of supply to Borneo was
from China, from which one or two large junks brought
each year iron lance-heads, swords, pots and pans, crockery,
copper goods, and silk. The Borneo traders also received
embroidered cloths from India. They exchanged these goods
in the western islands of the Philippines for gold, slaves,
certain shells which served in Siam and Sumatra for coinage,
cheap white Philippines cloth, cinnamon, ginger and wax.

The Borneo pilot also explained that Chinese junks plied directly between China and Luzon, the northern island of the Philippines, and that the traders of Luzon, being better able to traverse the dangerous waters of the Philippines than the large junks, distributed these goods to the eastern and southern islands in large canoes.

When Tuasan heard of the peculiar reactions of the islanders of Mazagua and Camiguin and Bohol at the approach of the Armada, he was able to solve the mystery. About two years previously, explained Tuasan, eight armed canoes of Moluccans, with a number of Spaniards, came and made friends with the people of Bohol. One day the visitors fell upon their hosts, slaughtered several hundred, including the leading chief, and carried off more than four hundred men, women and children into slavery. On the way back to the Moluccas they attacked and laid waste Mazagua. For this reason the people of Bohol and Mazagua and the neighbouring islands were terrified of the name of Spain.

The people on the flagship, when they heard this, explained that no Spaniards had been in those parts for twenty years, and that the Europeans who had come with the Moluccans must have been Portuguese. Legazpi and his associates had no doubt that the Portuguese had deliberately represented themselves as Spaniards on this foray against the people of Bohol.

The assistance of the Borneo pilot now proved invaluable, because he was able to interpret for them with the chiefs of Bohol. Their suspicions were set at rest when the pilot explained to them that the present visitors were of a different kingdom from those who had betrayed them two years previously.

The two principal local chiefs, Zicatuna and Zigala, now came to the flagship and drank blood and wine with Legazpi. They explained, however, that food was short at Bohol, because of a crop failure. Indeed they themselves were being obliged to get food from Zebu, the large fertile island which was in sight to the west from Bohol.

It was now decided to send the pinnace, under the command of a military officer named Juan de Aguirre, on an exploratory visit to Zebu. The chief pilot, Esteban Rodriguez, accompanied Aguirre as sailing-master. The Borneo pilot and the expedition's Malay-speaking interpreter went along also, so that when the former translated the Philippine speech into Malay, the latter could translate the Malay into Spanish. The pinnace went off with instructions to return from Zebu within eight days.

The eight days which had been set for the return of the pinnace from Zebu came and went, and still no sign of the vessel was seen. After Aguirre had been gone thirteen days, Zicatuna and Zigala, the two friendly chiefs of Bohol, agreed for a consideration in gold to go to Zebu in search of the missing pinnace. They accordingly set off in a large canoe, accompanied by two Spanish musketeers.

Legazpi's anxiety to make contact with Zebu did not arise solely from his desire to get supplies of food. Tuasan had told him that two Spaniards had been held captive by the islanders there, that one of these captives had been sold to some Borneo traders, and that the Portuguese in Borneo had ransomed him. Part of Legazpi's instructions enjoined him to try to seek out and rescue any survivors of past Spanish expeditions who might still be in the Isles of the West. In due course, as we shall see, one such survivor was in fact found and rescued under dramatic circumstances, although not in Zebu.

All these factors, therefore, influenced the Spaniards to turn their attention to Zebu. It was already well known to them by name and reputation from the accounts of Magellan's expedition. Another thing that made the situation propitious for a move to Zebu if the reports of it by Legazpi's emissaries proved encouraging was the completion of the repairs to the galleons at Bohol, where the flagship, the *San Pedro*, was given a new bowsprit, mainyard and mizzen-mast.

It was about this time that Arellano, Lope Martin and the little company of the *San Lucas* passed close to the galleons as it proceeded north. Whether Lope Martin and his cronies among the sailors saw the galleons may be an open question. Perhaps it was a case of ships that pass in the night.

6

Birth Pangs of Empire

THE early weeks of April 1565 were a worrying time for
Legazpi and his associates at Bohol. The *San Lucas* was nowhere to be found. They did not know that at that very time
it passed close to them, going on to anticipate their own hope
that the *San Pedro* would for the first time in history complete
the traverse of the Pacific from the Philippines to America.
Juan de la Isla was absent on a visit to Mindanao in the *San
Juan*. Juan de Aguirre had gone off with sixteen men in the
pinnace to Zebu with instructions to return in eight days,
and after he had been absent for thirteen days the Bohol
chiefs Zicatuna and Zigala had gone off in search of them.

One of Legazpi's anxieties was relieved when one day the
San Juan came sailing into the inlet to rejoin the two large
ships. Captain Isla had quite a tale to tell of their experiences
at Butuan, on the north coast of Mindanao. They found there
two large canoes of Moslems from Luzon, trading with the
people of Butuan. Isla paid his respects to the chief of
Butuan, giving him on behalf of Legazpi the velvet jacket
and cape that had been made for the chief of Mazagua. The
chief was, however, threatened later by the Luzon traders so
that he would not trade with the Spaniards. Some of these
traders came on board the *San Juan* and had a look at the
Spanish goods. They got very excited when they saw the
silver, and paid for some of it in gold, of which they had
considerable amounts. Isla also bought some wax from them,

but some of it turned out to have earth in the middle encased in the wax. When Isla taxed the Luzon traders with this deception, they said they had got the wax from the people of Butuan without knowing of the malpractice, but this was obviously untrue since all the wax at Butuan was in small pieces. The soldiers on the *San Juan* wanted to seize the traders' gold, saying they deserved to lose it because of their fraud. But Isla would not allow this, since he had been told not to mistreat any of the people he met.

When the people of the Armada at Bohol heard of the quantities of gold on the Luzon ships, numbers of them wanted to go and seize it, using as their pretext the deceit practised by the traders. But Legazpi, knowing that their motive was greed for the gold, would have none of this.

Some days later, Zicatuna and Zigala arrived back from Zebu, bringing the two Spanish musketeers safe and sound. They had asked the people along the east coast of Zebu whether they had seen or heard anything of Aguirre and the pinnace, but without result. The musketeers did, however, have some good news for Legazpi. Zebu Town, about half-way up the east coast of the island, had a fine natural haven, and the country around appeared fertile with much food. Zebu Town and the neighbouring villages were populous. Furthermore the people there had numbers of ornaments made of gold. Nowhere in the islands had the musketeers seen anywhere to touch Zebu Town.

Legazpi and the whole company were much put out to have no news of the pinnace. Since it had then been gone twenty-two days, they thought they must give it up for lost. Great joy was therefore felt when that very night it came into the inlet.

When Juan de Aguirre and Chief Pilot Esteban Rodriguez met with Legazpi and his officers to tell their story, the Borneo pilot, Tuasan, was not with them.

First Rodriguez, as befitted his profession, told of the course followed on the voyage. They had passed south of the island of Zebu and so arrived at the south of Los Negros, the island beyond Zebu to the west. They then tried to get back to Zebu, but the wind was dead against them and they found after a day they were farther west than when they started. They therefore had to run up the west coast of Los Negros and round the north of it, whereupon they saw Zebu to the east. They sailed down the west coast of Zebu, and since by that time they were long overdue, they returned direct to the galleons at Bohol.

The reason why Zicatuna and Zigala and the musketeers did not see or hear anything of the pinnace was thus explained. Whereas the chiefs had gone to Zebu Town on the east coast, Aguirre had never been on that side of Zebu Island.

Of the Borneo pilot, Aguirre had a sad story to tell. On the north coast of Los Negros, Tuasan had asked some of the people where there was water, and one man offered to take him to a watering-place. Tuasan accordingly went off with this fellow, with twelve Spaniards following with the casks and six muskets. When they came to the spring Tuasan bent down to drink. The man who had guided him then thrust a lance through his side before the very eyes of the watering-party, who ran to him only to find him dead and the assailant gone. Then a great number of warriors who had been lying in ambush in the trees burst out on them. The men with the muskets stood their ground and formed a ring, and fired their muskets into the thick of the attackers. One fell dead and others crawled away wounded. That was enough for the rest. They ran so fast that horses could not have kept up with them.

The Spaniards were all very grieved to hear of the death of Tuasan, who had been a great help to them and had become their friend.

Aguirre also had tales of adventure and other hairbreadth escapes. At one place they thought they would make a landing, but the local warriors gathered on the beach and shook their lances and knives, whereupon the pinnace passed on. Then farther on they were just about to land when at least five hundred men who had apparently been stalking them suddenly burst out of the trees, thinking to have the pinnace at their mercy. But Gunner Pedro de Solorzano fired the two culverins in the bow of the pinnace to such good effect that the attackers turned tail and fled. Then near the south point of Zebu, when the Spaniards were down to only a few beans as the daily ration, they met some fishermen who seemed friendly and gave them some fish, telling them to wait while they went to their village and brought more food. After an hour they came back with some coconuts and fish and wine, which they offered almost for nothing. Aguirre and his companions had their suspicions and made the men drink some of it themselves. They took it in their mouths but were in due course observed to spit it out. Some of the Spaniards wanted to kill them for their treachery, but Aguirre let them go.

Not all the stories that the voyagers in the pinnace had to tell of their experiences were as grim as those Aguirre recounted. At one place the pinnace came on a large canoe with about twenty-five men, women and children aboard. The canoe immediately put in to the shore and the occupants fled. When the Spaniards got to the canoe they found a pretty little Philippine girl, about three years old, clinging to the side of the canoe with her body in the water, crying bitterly. As they approached she let go her grip, and would have been drowned if one of the men in the pinnace had not leapt in the water and rescued her. He brought her into the pinnace, where they comforted her and gave her something to eat. Then they put her back in the canoe, leaving it and her for the terrified owners to find again.

At another place, at night, a canoe was heard approaching, the paddlers calling the stroke according to their custom. The people in the canoe got a great surprise when they found themselves alongside the pinnace. When they asked who the Spaniards were, the Borneo pilot told them they were Chinese. 'That's a lie', came the answer, 'the China junks are quite different from your craft, and we'll make war on you at dawn.' This spirited reply was received with jollity and laughter by the Spaniards, who told the Borneo pilot to tell the Filipinos they wanted to be friends.

At dawn the Spaniards bore down on the canoe, which then made for the shore faster than a galley. In due course the Borneo pilot managed to reassure the people on shore, who came around the pinnace. As ill chance would have it, however, the wind then blew and removed the cover under which the two culverins in the bow of the pinnace were hidden. At the sight of their menacing shapes the villagers immediately took to flight.

Everybody at Bohol was now agreed that they should go to Zebu Town and make a settlement there. So the three ships set sail from Bohol on 22 April. This was the day that the *San Lucas* finally set out for Mexico.

After a passage of several days because of calms, the three ships of the Armada came to anchor close to the populous settlement of Zebu Town, on the east coast of Zebu Island.

Here the voyagers found a port which answered to their hopes. It was an inlet across the mouth of which lay the island of Mactan, making a natural haven with a north and a south entrance. The ships were able to anchor close to the native town, which consisted of some three hundred huts. The luxuriant verdure showed the fertility of the soil, and pigs, fowls, goats and cultivations could be seen in abundance.

On the beach were a number of villagers. Legazpi called for Pacheco, the interpreter, and asked him to try to make the people understand that they came in peace, and wished their chief to come on board to a parley.

Pacheco called out to the people in a mixture of Malay and their own language. Apparently they understood what was asked of them, for after a time a man came on board, saying he was there on behalf of the chief, whose name was Tupas. He said that Tupas would come to the ship later, and asked that the artillery and muskets be kept away, since the islanders were afraid of them. The envoy then returned to the shore with some trifles for himself, and with the promise of a fine present for Tupas when he came aboard.

The people of Zebu Town had good cause to know a Spanish expedition when they saw one. It was in the time of Tupas's father, when Tupas himself was a boy, that Magellan had been killed on Mactan and over a score of his associates massacred in Zebu Town itself.

An hour or two after Tupas's envoy had gone ashore, an old Borneo Moslem who was living at Zebu came aboard, saying that he was fluent both in Malay and the local language and had been sent by Tupas as an interpreter. Tupas and the other chiefs, he assured Legazpi, were preparing to come on board. The Borneo Moslem then went ashore again.

Some time later, however, it was seen that the people on shore were loading their gear and retreating into the surrounding country or going along the coast in canoes.

It was debated whether force should be used to stop the evacuation, but Legazpi was determined to exhaust the ways of peace.

Legazpi waited all the next day for Tupas to appear, but in vain.

The feelings of Tupas concerning an invitation to go on board the flagship may be gauged from what had happened to the Spaniards of Magellan's expedition who had been killed by Tupas's father. They had been invited to a feast with malice aforethought. One of them was spared by his assassins long enough to go down to the beach and plead to his comrades on the ships to ransom him. He shouted out to them that twenty-four of the twenty-six men who had accepted the chief's invitation had been massacred, whereupon the Spaniards in the ships, judging that discretion was the better part of valour, sailed off leaving him to his fate. Tupas no doubt felt that the positions might well be reversed, with himself as the victim, if he now delivered himself into Legazpi's power.

The next day Saz and Urdaneta went in close to the beach in a boat and gave messages for Tupas exhorting him to come within two hours, but although Tupas sent a message that he would do so, after considerably more than the allowed time there was no sign of him. So in went Saz and Urdaneta to the beach again, with a further message that if Tupas did not come within two hours he must bear the consequences. This time a man claiming to be one of Tupas's captains offered to come in place of the chief, but Saz said that only Tupas's presence would suffice. Saz also offered to leave hostages on shore for Tupas's safety. It was plain, however, that Tupas was merely playing for time, since while these conferences were going on, the villagers continued hastily to remove their goods and livestock. Yet a third time Legazpi sent Saz and Urdaneta to the shore, this time with an ultimatum for Tupas to come. Now, however, the reception was different, for the evacuation was by this time completed. Tupas's warriors, waving their lances, knives and bows, shouted defiance from the beach, and ten or twelve large canoes bringing reinforcements from neighbouring villages were observed. It was estimated that the forces ranged against the Spaniards comprised 1500 to 2000 men.

After Saz and Urdaneta got back to the flagship, Legazpi had a consultation with the officers, monks and Crown

officials. He asked them if it were not true that he had done
everything possible to win these people over to the renewal
of the allegiance to Spain that they had acknowledged in
Magellan's time, whereas they had shown themselves
perfidious and intractable.

It was unanimously agreed that patience had been tried to
the breaking point and that stronger measures were now
justified.

Legazpi and his captains now drew up their battle plan.
The pinnace and the ships' boats were loaded with 200 men
in all, some being deputed to go against the canoes, and
others against the settlement. As a preliminary to these
assault waves, the artillery on the flagship fired on the canoes,
while the guns of the *San Pablo* and the *San Juan* bombarded
the town.

In the face of the roar of the guns, and the spectacular
effect of the shot falling in the water and among the huts, the
canoes and the warriors on shore made no fight of it. They
turned and retreated with nimble feet, and the soldiers who
pursued them were soon left far behind. The result was:
casualties nil, prisoners ditto.

Legazpi's satisfaction with his bloodless victory was soon
overcome by a fresh anxiety. Smoke and flames were seen
rising in the middle of the village. The dry and inflammable
thatch of one of the huts, ignited by a shot from the bom-
bardment, had caught on fire. The flames spread from hut to
hut in spectacular fashion, and did not stop until some
hundred huts had been destroyed.

The Spaniards were now in undisputed possession of the
deserted and half-burned village, but all they found were a
few household articles, apart from one remarkable discovery.
A sailor named Juan de Camuz was poking round in a particularly humble little hut, when he saw a pinewood chest
among some rubbish in a corner. When it was opened, it

D

was found to contain a small statue of the Infant Jesus in a dress and hat, in good order except that the little cross on the orb in the Infant's hand was broken off. It was an image such as was made contemporarily in Flanders.

When this dramatic find was shown to the devout Legazpi, he was deeply moved. Hernan Riquel, the scribe, recorded the Captain-General's very words. Taking the image in his hands Legazpi kissed its feet, and raising his eyes to Heaven, said: 'Lord, Thou art powerful to punish the offences done in this isle against Thy Majesty, and in order to found in it Thy House and Holy Church where Thy glorious name may be venerated and exalted, I beseech that Thou enlighten and guide me so that all that we do here may be to Thy glory and honour, and glorification of Thy Holy Catholic Faith.'

It was accordingly decided by the monks that their proposed church would have the name of Jesus.

The statue, it was generally agreed, was a relic of the visit of Magellan's expedition.

Over the next week or two Saz and the other captains headed expeditions to the villages in the vicinity of Zebu Town, finding them deserted. They foraged for such food as the inhabitants had left. At one place they found two men, one of them wounded, and two old women, and took them on board one of the ships, but the very same night they disappeared over the side without being seen. At one village the soldiers were suddenly attacked by three hundred warriors who were hiding nearby, but the assailants, as usual, could not withstand the muskets and soon fled.

At night, however, the roles were reversed, and the soldiers became the hunted. They had been disembarked from the ships and lodged in the village, four men to a hut. Sentinels were posted each night. But because the palm groves in and around the village were thick, the attackers were able to creep up close to the sentinels without being

seen, and fling darts and lances at them. Nor was it possible
to catch the assailants, for they disappeared into the jungle
as quickly as they came, and knew the paths. As a result of
the commotions which were thus raised by the raiders every
night, the soldiers on shore got very little sleep. Nor could
they be shifted back to the ships, because there was much
work to be done all day and every day in consolidating the
settlement.

The classical answer to this sort of situation is of course a
high wooden palisade. The construction of one was now
begun under Saz's supervision. It took the form of a triangle,
the three points of which were marked out with due ceremony. Possession of Zebu was taken in the name of Spain.

At this time Legazpi was sleeping on the *San Pedro*, because
the orders of the Real Audiencia were that he do this until
he was sure that it was safe for him to remove to shore. But
during the day he came ashore to push the work along,
expecting everybody, no matter what his station, to take a
hand, and setting the pace himself.

The very same night that the palisade was commenced,
Saz and his soldiers in the village, worn out with the day's
toil, were suddenly awakened by a great hubbub as the Zebu
warriors made one of their customary attacks on the camp.
This time, however, the assailants were more than ordinarily
successful. When Saz got to the door of his hut, he saw that
several of the huts were ablaze, throwing prolific sparks onto
the thatch of the others. The guards explained that the
assailants had staged a diversionary attack at one side of the
camp, and when the guards had gone there the arsonists
on the other side managed to get a conflagration going in
several of the empty huts. By the time the soldiers had got
the spreading flames under control, many huts had gone up
in smoke.

In the morning Legazpi and the officers had a council.

Legazpi said that they must shift all their gear and supplies
into a protected area in an earth store-house so that they
would be out of danger of fire.

All the huts except those which were occupied were
demolished, and the equipment and food were concentrated
according to Legazpi's plan.

One day Guido de la Bezares, the treasurer, made a
complaint to Legazpi. The Crown officials were responsible
for seeing that the King's Treasury received one-fifth of any
gold or other precious metal that might be found, for that
was the standing levy throughout the Empire. Bezares
reported that numbers of soldiers had been going round the
villages opening up the burial places of the natives. There
they had found many valuable gold pendants, bracelets, ear-
rings and anklets, for it was the custom of the people to bury
such things with their dead. But the soldiers had then secreted
these finds without declaring them.

It was accordingly decided that the soldiers should be
warned against robbing the graves in this way and hiding the
loot. The reason for the concern shown over this was shown
when, at Legazpi's order, the drummer Hippolyto, with the
scribe Hernan Riquel as witness, took up his stand in the
centre of the camp and rolled on his drum to attract the
attention of the men. He then read out the edict in a loud
voice. Everybody, he announced, who took gold and other
precious things from the graves of the natives must register
them with the Crown officials and give up one-fifth of the
value thereof to the Royal Treasury, or be under penalty
of forfeiting the lot.

This shows that it was not considered bad form to rob the
burial places of the infidels. Any gold that was found there
was fair loot, provided the due fifth was paid to the King.

It will be remembered that the sailors and soldiers who
had found gold in the Borneo ship at Bohol had argued that

this was fair loot. Loot, it appears very plainly in history, has always bulked large in the minds of conquerors and their followers. Hernan Riquel's note of the edict which Hippolyto the drummer proclaimed in Zebu gives a glimpse of the pickings which were available in the Philippines.

Preparations were now well forward for sending the *San Pedro* on its apparently vital task of finding a way of sailing directly east to Mexico. The Captain-General's grandson, Felipe de Salcedo, was to go as captain, and Urdaneta was to retire from the expedition after accompanying Salcedo. They did not know that the *San Lucas* was already well on the way ahead of them.

Urdaneta had the satisfaction of consecrating the Church of the Infant Jesus as one of his final contributions to the expedition. He and his five brother monks had stood aside from the military part of the expedition's proceedings in Zebu. Their hopes for the Christianizing of the people of Zebu were bound up in the little church that was built at a distance from the military quarters. Its construction had been one of the first things embarked on after the landing.

Legazpi commanded that all the camp should follow the monks to the church from the hut where the Image of the Infant Jesus had been found. On the day appointed the monks set out from the hut holding the Image on high, with Legazpi and the captains and the Crown officials and the gentlemen and soldiers following. On the way the procession was met by two visiting chiefs and their followers, who showed by their lack of arms that they were seeking peace. Legazpi, much encouraged by this good omen, invited them to join the procession to the church.

The whole company, including the chiefs and their retinue, continued on to the church and entered it with great solemnity. The Image was placed upon the altar and adored. Then Mass was celebrated, followed by a sermon of thanks and praise. A Brotherhood of the Holy Name of Jesus was founded according to the rules of the Augustinians of Mexico. All of this was observed with much awe by the watching chiefs and their followers.

The trouble caused by the people in and around Tupas's territory had now fallen off considerably. Legazpi let it be known that no vengeance would be taken on any who came in peace, and was obviously keeping his word with the lesser visitors.

One day a brother of Tupas came with an offer to make friendship and drink blood and wine with Legazpi. When Legazpi asked why Tupas himself did not come, the chief said that Tupas was some distance away but would be back in two or three days. Legazpi bade him tell Tupas to come in peace and no harm would befall him. Saz, as second-in-command, then deputized for Legazpi in drinking blood and wine with the chief. Legazpi gave his visitor a finely-worked cloth and said that this should be held high on a staff as a sign of peace when the chief came in sight of the camp, and that any of the people of Zebu who similarly used a white flag in their comings and goings would be unmolested.

Four or five days passed, and during this time many of the Zebu people came to the camp or passed freely in their canoes, always with a white flag as their passport and evidence of their good intentions. Every day the Captain-General made known that he wanted Tupas himself to come and seal the peace, and that no harm would come to him.

Finally came the day when Tupas presented himself for the first time in person, attended by forty or fifty followers. With him were two Malay-speaking Moslems as interpreters.

Legazpi received Tupas with much honour, saying that the King of Spain desired that the people of Zebu should acknowledge their allegiance to him, whereupon he would protect and cherish them. Since blood had been spilt in the previous few weeks, as in Captain-General Magellan's time, it was right and proper that Tupas and his people should make amends by paying tribute in token amounts of gold and food. Tupas was accordingly bidden to come back on the third day thereafter with this tribute, when Legazpi would have a treaty of friendship and mutual help for them to accept together.

Tupas agreed with every appearance of willingness to these terms, and Legazpi and Tupas and another leading chief then drew blood from their chests with daggers into a cup of wine which was divided into three parts and drunk with due ceremony. After that the two chiefs ate with Legazpi and his senior officers and then went ashore, Tupas assuring his hosts that he would be back in three days.

The three days went by, and during this time peace reigned in Zebu Town. The local fishermen resumed their occupation, making a picturesque sight at night as they worked in the light of torches. The villages in the vicinity of the port were reoccupied.

Three days more went by, however, with no signs of Tupas and his fellow chiefs. Having found one of Tupas's interpreters, Legazpi asked him why Tupas did not come. The interpreter answered that it was because Tupas was having difficulty in gathering the tribute as commanded by Legazpi. Legazpi then bade the interpreter tell Tupas that that was no good reason for not coming to conclude the treaty as arranged.

Actually the people of the villages which were not in direct contact with the Spaniards were at this time inciting Tupas not to co-operate with the foreign invaders. In particular the chiefs of Gavi and Mactan were inclined to be contemptuous of the Spaniards and of Tupas for suffering them. Mactan had had the distinction of repulsing and killing Magellan. Dagami, the chief of Gavi, was a particularly troublesome fellow, noted for making mischief among the Zebu villages. The

recalcitrant chiefs of Gavi and Mactan were all for harrying
the Spaniards and denying them food so as to force them to
evacuate.

Dagami now conspired with four other chiefs to lay an
ambush on the outskirts of the Spanish camp. Dagami
accordingly led a party of eighteen warriors along the coast
in a canoe. They hid in a thicket on the edge of the beach
not far from the gate of the camp. No longer could they make
the swift attacks and retreats which had forced the Spaniards
to erect the palisade round the camp, but they still hoped to
pick off any of Legazpi's men who might come within
striking distance.

Now at dawn next day, Pedro de Arana, one of Legazpi's
company of gentlemen, announced to a friend that it would
be pleasant to go for a stroll outside the camp along the beach.
The friend warned Arana that it was forbidden by the Captain-
General to go out of the camp without a proper guard, and
that the recent falling off in the friendship of the local people
was a warning in itself. But Arana insisted that he would be
quite safe, saying that he would take a musket in case of
trouble.

The foolhardy Arana went out of the camp and along the
beach, little knowing the dreadful fate that awaited him.
When he came opposite the ambush, Dagami's warriors
burst out on him with frightful yells, flinging their lances
at him. Before he had time to use his musket they had struck
him down. Then they swiftly cut off his head as a trophy, got
into their canoe, and were seen paddling off along the coast.

When this sad news was brought to Legazpi, he felt that
Heaven must have forsaken him for his sins. It was now a
month after the arrival of the Armada at Zebu Town, and
he had got nowhere in securing the co-operation of the
islanders. His men were pinned down and continually

hungry. Was his expedition to suffer the fate of those of Magellan and Villalobos and come to disaster?

Legazpi called Saz and Goite, the military commanders, to a conference. He said that if the people of Zebu wanted war, war they should have. It was arranged that Legazpi should sleep ashore in the camp under the guard of his company of gentlemen that night, so that the captains might take all the soldiers they could muster and go after the assassins.

Legazpi, for the first time, slept in the camp that night, the gentlemen being divided into four watches to keep guard. The officer of the watch had quite a deal of bother with some of the haughty dons, who refused to take their turn on watch because it was the work of common soldiers. He did not, however, trouble the sleeping Captain-General with the report of this disloyalty.

Meanwhile Captain Saz and Captain Goite had gone along the coast in the ships' boats with a full complement of soldiers, following the direction taken by the assassins' canoe. In the meantime Dagami and his associates had left the canoe at a small village along the coast and gone off with Arana's head to Gavi, where they enjoyed a feast in fierce triumph over their exploit. When Saz and Goite came to the place where the canoe had been left, their men found it with Arana's blood still fresh upon it. The Spaniards burnt the dozen or so huts at this place, and took back captive to the camp the few people whom they found there.

Among the captives whom Saz brought back to the camp were two women and two girls. The two girls proved to be the daughters of one of Tupas's brothers, named Simaquio, one of the women captives being Simaquio's wife, the girls' mother. The generous Legazpi ordered that the women and girls be put in one of the huts in the camp and treated well, intending to return them to their people in due course.

The morning after these various excitements, the dons who had refused to stand watch during the night complained in no uncertain terms of the attempted indignity. Two of them in particular, Pedro de Mena and Esteban Terra, were loudly voluble in protest at the attempt to make them do the duty of common soldiers.

When Saz heard of their recalcitrance he decided to discipline them. At this time the flagship was ready to sail for Mexico, and the lists of those who would return in the ship and those who would remain and serve at Zebu were being made out. Saz gave orders that the trouble-makers should be included in those who would remain. The disaffected gentlemen took this very badly, and retired for the night in high dudgeon.

In the middle of the night the watch in the camp raised an alarm that a building was on fire. This was the building in which the lists of those who were returning to Mexico and those who were remaining at Zebu were held. Alongside it was the building where Legazpi kept his private property, and another building containing official ammunition and equipment. All of these were in considerable danger. The efforts of the fire-fighters, however, were successful in arresting the fire before it destroyed any of the buildings completely.

When the building which had been the source of the fire was inspected, something startling was found. It was obvious that incendiary material had been deliberately put in the thatch. When Saz investigated this attempted arson, there was no doubt who the culprits were. Before the sun was high in the sky the following morning, Pedro de Mena and Esteban Terra were swinging from the gallows.

As the *San Pedro* sailed from Zebu on 1 June, 1565, leaving the *San Pablo* as Legazpi's new flagship, the scribe Hernan Riquel closed the official report to the Real Audiencia in Mexico City with the following words: 'Not only are there enemies without, but in the camp itself, who being disaffected can make greater mischief than house-thieves, from all which it will be appreciated how necessary and desirable it is that help come quickly from New Spain.' We shall see in a later chapter that the most dangerous rebels were not in the camp, but in the *San Pablo*, and were not gentlemen of Spain.

7
Mutiny on the High Seas

GREAT hopes were placed by Legazpi and his officers at Zebu in the attempt to sail the *San Pedro* back from the Philippines across the North Pacific to Mexico. There were three good reasons why Legazpi should be particularly concerned that the *San Pedro* should be successful on this journey. The first was that, as the King of Spain himself had made plain, a direct two-way communication between Mexico and the Isles of the West was necessary if the settlement at Zebu was to be made good, for the access from the west was in Portuguese hands. Secondly the expedition at Zebu was in great need of supplies, ammunition and other help. Thirdly the Viceroy of New Spain, Don Luis Velasco, before his death, had encouraged Legazpi to think that if the problem of getting back direct to Mexico were solved, Legazpi might expect a reward of 4000 ducats from the King. This reward would have meant a lot to Legazpi, for he had impoverished himself in preparing for the expedition. In a letter to the King which went with the *San Pedro*, Legazpi raised the matter of a reward for his services.

Legazpi did not know at this time that the missing *San Lucas*, at the time when the *San Pedro* sailed from Zebu on 1 June, 1565, was half-way across the Pacific on its journey to Mexico. Had Legazpi known this, he might have been doubly anxious, since it would not be the best of recommendations for a reward to him if Arellano in the *San Lucas* forestalled him. Legazpi's conclusion was that Arellano had deliberately defected from the Armada early in the voyage from Mexico and had returned to New Spain. On that assumption, he sent representations with the *San Pedro* to the Real Audiencia in Mexico City, asking that Arellano be sent to Zebu with the *San Lucas* to answer Legazpi's charge and to make the ship available to Legazpi for much-needed service.

Legazpi's grandson Felipe de Salcedo went as captain of the *San Pedro* with his kinsman Andres de Urdaneta as mentor. The chief pilot was Esteban Rodriguez. The plotter Pierres Plun, the erstwhile second pilot of the *San Pedro*, remained at Zebu. The full company on the *San Pedro*, including crew, soldiers, monks and gentlemen, was two hundred.

After coming out of the inner sea of the Philippines through San Bernardino Strait, the *San Pedro* in due course quitted the Philippines and bore north-east into the vast expanses of the North Pacific.

On 21 June the *San Pedro* came to a ring of reefs and rocks enclosing a lagoon, which from a distance they thought was a sailing ship. This was the isolated drowned atoll bearing to this day the name Parece Vela, meaning 'Sail in sight'.

Continuing on to the north-east, the *San Pedro* increased its latitude until it reached as far north as 39 degrees, much as the *San Lucas* had done a couple of months previously. The *San Pedro* thus got the benefit of the Japan Current and the westerlies of higher latitudes on its way to North America, as the *San Lucas* had done. The toll of disease was even greater than on the *San Lucas*, and before the journey was over, sixteen of the ship's company were consigned to the sea. Eventually, on 18 September, 1565, the *San Pedro* came to one of the islands near the site of the modern Los Angeles, a few centuries too early to appear in pictures.

As they were running down the Mexico coast, the chief pilot, Esteban Rodriguez, was removed from the *San Pedro* by death. He had at least had the satisfaction of taking the great galleon from Mexico to the Philippines and back again, and did not know he had been anticipated by Lope Martin.

The *San Pedro* passed La Navidad without entering the port, and on 8 October, 1565, sailed into Acapulco.

During the two months that elapsed between the arrival of the *San Lucas* and that of the *San Pedro* in Mexico, Arellano, Lope Martin and the company of the *San Lucas* had been welcomed in Mexico City as heroes, as indeed they were. They told the story of how they had reached the Philippines, had waited at Mindanao for more than a month, and had then traversed the Philippines from south to north without seeing any sign of the Armada. It looked therefore very much as if some disaster had overtaken the main expedition. One thing was certain, that the *San Lucas* had found a way of getting back direct to North America. This was momentous, because it established that a new Spanish empire in the Isles of the West was viable so far as the vital matter of communication was concerned. The Real Audiencia gave consideration to the matter of a reward to Arellano.

When Salcedo and Urdaneta heard that Arellano and Lope Martin had claimed to have gone to the Philippines and back again, they did not believe that the *San Lucas* could in fact have traversed the Philippines looking for the Armada. They made haste to Mexico City.

Great was the joy of Legazpi's family, and of Felipe de Salcedo's father Pedro, and of the monks of the Order of St Augustine, over the safe return of Felipe and Urdaneta, and the reassuring news that Legazpi was alive at Zebu.

The matter of making good the charges against Arellano now engaged the attention of Legazpi's associates. Their spokesman was Gabriel Diaz, the treasurer in the Royal

Mint at Mexico City, who was later to back with his own money Salcedo's return to Zebu in support of Legazpi. Legazpi had sent in the *San Pedro* an empowerment to Diaz to lay an information with the authorities in Mexico City, supported by a sworn statement by the captains and pilots of the three ships at Zebu. This statement accused Arellano of having deliberately absconded from the fleet. It cited the fact that although Captain Juan de la Isla had told the pilot Lope Martin to keep only half a league ahead of the flagship, the *San Lucas* had in fact persisted in going a long way ahead, and that when Arellano had been hailed and reproved for this, Lope Martin had called back saying that he could not shorten sail and lose way in a cross-sea because of the low sides of the vessel. The information went on to say that after the *San Lucas* disappeared, no cross or message was found by the Armada at any of the islands visited by it, and that nothing of the *San Lucas* was heard of at any of the islands in the Philippines. It was therefore requested that Arellano be sent with the *San Lucas* to Zebu to answer Legazpi's charge and make available the ship.

In due course Arellano gave the authorities a written statement, signed and sworn to by himself and Lope Martin, giving in great detail the course and events of their journey. Since Diaz could not produce a similar statement from Legazpi and his officers to match that of Arellano, the case failed, and Arellano was allowed to proceed to Spain.

On the basis of the accusations of Legazpi and his supporters, Arellano, no less than Lope Martin, has been branded in history as a conspirator and wilful deserter. Those who made the charge did not have the benefit of the knowledge which we have today. The itinerary of the *San Lucas* can be established in detail from the copious topographical descriptions in Arellano's account. The course of the *San Lucas* was by way of islands of which the topography was not known in

detail for several centuries later. There can therefore be no
doubt of the authenticity of the track of the *San Lucas*. The
San Lucas struck the Philippines in latitude 9 degrees, whereas
Urdaneta persuaded Legazpi to go up to Guam in 13 degrees,
whence they reached the Philippines in 12 degrees, so that it
was in fact Legazpi who departed from the latitudes in
which, in accordance with the instructions of the Real
Audiencia, the greater part of the traverse of the Pacific from
Mexico was made. The peculiar manoeuvrings of the *San
Lucas* at the time of its disappearance are no evidence against
Arellano, being entirely compatible with Lope Martin's
proved intrigues, and it was in fact against Martin alone that
the initial suspicion of desertion was directed according to
the entry at the time in the official report. Pedro de Rivero,
the second-in-command of the *San Lucas*, and other Spaniards
on board the *San Lucas* must all have been great knaves or
great fools if Arellano were guilty of wilful desertion.
Arellano himself must have been a remarkable fool if he had
signed a false statement which could have been blown out
by any one of a dozen participants in the voyage. There is no
reason for thinking that Arellano knew anything of a reward
for the return voyage. This was merely a promise made by
Don Luis the Viceroy, specifically to Legazpi, and subject
to the consent of the King. Just what motive Arellano might
have had for subjecting himself to the dangers and privations
of a separate voyage in a tiny vessel if his defection were
deliberate is hard to see. The magistrates of the Real
Audiencia would also have been taking a grave risk in
ignoring Legazpi's representations if they felt that a further
inquiry might possibly uphold the accusations.

Legazpi and his supporters continued to ask the King of
Spain for a reward for making the return journey, but no
reward appears ever to have been paid either to Legazpi or
Arellano.

The *San Pedro* had brought a cargo of gold, spices and other wares from the Philippines for the King of Spain himself. The ship went on to Spain to deliver them, and to enlist help there for Legazpi.

Andres de Urdaneta now passes out of our story. He had seen the fulfilment of his role of guide, philosopher and friend to Legazpi in the establishment of the settlement and the successful return of the *San Pedro* to Mexico and Spain. He returned to Mexico from Spain in due course, and devoted the few remaining years of his life to the service of the Augustinian Order from which the King's commission had temporarily taken him.

Lope Martin was for some unknown reason in custody in Mexico for a short time a few months after the return of the *San Pedro*. There is no reason to think that this was because his plotting had been discovered, since one might think that the gravity of attempted mutiny, if known, would have brought a graver penalty. Lope Martin was born to be in mischief, as the spectacular saga of the *San Jeronimo* will show.

When Legazpi's urgent plea for help came with the *San Pedro* to the Real Audiencia, the bureaucrats of Mexico City made some attempt to meet it without too great a delay. Their performance in preparing the Armada had not been impressive, for the captains and pilots had signed a joint complaint of the inadequacy and poor quality of the sails, rigging and other gear. The Mexico officials, however, managed to get some soldiers and supplies together and provide a small galleon, the *San Jeronimo*, which was so old that it later had to be broken up in the Philippines.

As captain of the *San Jeronimo* the authorities appointed one Pero Sanchez Pericon, and as ensign went his son Pericon Mesa.

The Pericons set out from Mexico City with a small company of fifty soldiers for Acapulco on the west coast, where they were to pick up some more soldiers and embark on the *San Jeronimo*. At Chilapa, on the way to Acapulco, they remained for forty days, filling in time because of delays in getting the ship ready at Acapulco.

A dramatic and moving account of the march to the coast and the voyage of the *San Jeronimo* was recorded by one of the soldiers, Juan Martinez.

Martinez's opinion of the Pericons was of a forbidding nature. Captain Pericon was 'a miserable melancholic enemy of kindness and friend of envious solitude although we gave him the reputation of being a Christian since he was devout in prayer. He was the friend of his own opinion and judgment and not so prudent as his position demanded.' As for Pericon's son, he was a 'youth of 25 years and much more of a boy in discretion than years for he certainly always behaved in such fashion as to be a party to and reason for the evils which ensued both to us and to himself and his father, as his father had foretold, saying to him many times "You will be the death of me, so frequent are your misdeeds." '

The Pericons beguiled the time in Chilapa by having an elaborate gallows built to show the soldiers that they would stand no nonsense. They had a victim to hand to make an example of, in the person of a soldier who had wounded another in a quarrel. He was tried and hanged.

Eventually the Pericons and the soldiers got to Acapulco, where the galleon, the *San Jeronimo*, awaited them. They found that the pilot was one Lope Martin. The name meant nothing to them then.

After a while the gossip of the port came to Martinez's ears. He heard that Lope Martin and his captain, named Arellano, were reputed to have deserted from Legazpi's Armada. It was also said that they had thrown two men overboard in mid-ocean somewhere on the voyage.

As the days went by, more tales of Lope Martin's intrigues

came to the soldiers' notice. It was said that in selecting Lope Martin as pilot of the *San Jeronimo* the authorities were aiming to kill two birds with one stone, since charges against Martin could be investigated by Legazpi on the spot in Zebu after the *San Jeronimo* reached there.

After a while ominous reports of Martin's activities in Acapulco reached the ears of some of the officials themselves. It was said that in selecting the crew of the *San Jeronimo* the pilot was choosing as many of his own cronies as possible. For one thing he was taking seamen from his own neighbourhood in the south and rejecting Biscayans, who were not so likely to serve his ends. He was even giving jobs to Portuguese in preference to Spaniards. His old Portuguese friend Juan Jañiz was one. Lope Martin for his part, when he knew that his goings-on were attracting some notice, pressed for the early departure of the *San Jeronimo*, arguing that if delay took place the winds of the Pacific would be adverse for the passage.

One story, perhaps with some element of wisdom after the event, was put down by Martinez, in the very words Lope Martin was supposed to have used to Captain Pericon: 'Señor, if you think you can get me to Zebu you've another think coming, because within the hour of seeing me the Governor there would string me up. If, however, you changed your mind I could take you where you could get enough spoils to make you one of the richest men in Spain, I mean to Japan. You could make more than 200,000 ducats to add lustre to your line. I could take you to Mindanao to the Cape of Cinnamon, where you could establish your son in a fort with the soldiers. Then I would bring you through the Strait of Magellan to Spain, or else to Mexico, because the Governor Miguel Lopez de Legazpi is faced with ruin and you could get his job.'

The *San Jeronimo* set out from Acapulco on 1 May, 1566, the full complement of sailors and soldiers being 170.

The ship came south-west to latitude 9 degrees and was then becalmed for ten days. Someone said that two or three ships which had tried to go direct from Mexico to Peru instead of following the coast had never been heard of again, and suggested that perhaps they had been becalmed and everyone on board had died.

This cheerless thought produced a remarkable access of religious feeling among the virtuous and villainous alike. It was universally agreed that a collection should be taken up for the purpose of giving alms in the name of Our Lady of Consolation if they were delivered. Some gave 25 reals, others 10 to 20 pesos, and some a gold mark.

During this time two men died of boils and dysentery, which were widespread afflictions among the ship's company. Quick as a wink, as soon as they expired, the crew put them overboard. Nor in their extremity were these soldiers given any of the fowl or wine which remained. Rations had been fixed for the soldiers, but Martinez noted that the sailors were privileged and ate anything they liked.

One night a comet with varied hues flashed across the sky. This was regarded as a sign of evils done and miseries to come.

By this time Lope Martin had found his evil genius in the person of Felipe del Campo, one of the soldiers. Campo was a cunning fellow who knew how to manage Lope Martin. A sailor named Bartolomé de Lara, a wild excitable character, completed the main triumvirate of conspirators. Others there were who were well suited to play the part of jackals to these lions.

Lope Martin, like everybody else on board, took a dislike to the Pericons.

One day a wind which would have assisted the ship back to the American coast arose. Lope Martin wanted to take it, thinking that by getting back to land he and his fellow-conspirators might get an opportunity to steal the ship. The soldiers, being unused to the sea and its terrors, wanted to go back merely in order to get to dry land and stay there. Captain Pericon knew he would be deserted by most of his soldiers if he turned back. A day or two later, however, the dilemma was resolved by a change of wind, and soon the *San Jeronimo* was sailing steadily to the west in latitude 9 degrees.

Now Captain Pericon had a horse quartered in the bow of the ship. Of this horse he was very fond. One day Lope Martin had a talk with his co-conspirators. He told them he hated the Pericons and their horse too. Nor, said Lope, was it right that a horse should drink water while men went thirsty.

Pericon knew there had been grumbling about the watering of the horse when liquid was in short supply for the soldiers and crew. He therefore ordered that a guard be posted on the horse in its quarters in the prow. The soldiers grumbled when the order was conveyed, saying that anyone would think they were stable-boys.

A few nights later, the guards in the horse's quarters were awakened by the sound of retreating footsteps, but could not see who it was in the poor light. They found that blood was flowing as from a spout from a mortal dagger wound in the horse's heart.

The next day Santiago de Garnica, the ship's constable, received some information which made him go quickly to Pericon's cabin. Garnica told Pericon that he had news that Pilot Lope Martin and his friend Felipe del Campo had got the chief sergeant and the sergeant of the soldiers to join them in a conspiracy to leave the Pericons somewhere in the Philippines and take the ship off on a fortune-hunting expedition. They were reported to have a number of the ship's company in league with them.

This information was true. The chief sergeant was an old
soldier named Ortiz de Mosquera. Lope Martin's ally Felipe
del Campo, a soldier himself, had worked on Mosquera's
dislike of the Pericons and his envy of young Pericon's
position until he had Mosquera believing that it was his
duty to displace them. The sergeant, Pero Nuñez de
Solorzano, had followed Mosquera in this defection.

Now when a policeman makes an accusation of so serious
a character, it would seem common sense either to act
resolutely at once or else bide one's time. Pericon was,
however, apparently not a man of sense. He issued a procla-
mation to the effect that it had come to his notice that certain
persons were plotting against the King and himself, that
1000 pesos would be paid to anyone who testified against
them, and that 400 ducats would be given by him to anyone
who revealed the identity of the assassin of the horse.

Pericon thus put the plotters on notice that someone had
informed against them, and made them suspect Garnica of
having passed on the information.

This same day a great number of birds was seen. It was
thought that there must be a great land to the south, and the
course was directed to it. Lope Martin said it would be the
Isles of Solomon, of legendary fame. Excitement mounted
high as indistinct outlines in the southern sky proclaimed
the presence of this land. Pericon's son, the ensign, being
apparently no less inept than his father, announced out loud
that when they got to the land he would find out who killed
the horse and hang him. When Lope Martin heard this he
quietly changed course again to the west. Not that Lope
Martin was really in danger of finding the Isles of Solomon
and being hanged there, for there was no land in that part of
the Pacific Ocean.

By this time the Pericons had placed themselves in grave
jeopardy. They had forfeited the goodwill of soldiers and

sailors alike, and had raised a powerful cabal against them. The number of conspirators was now twelve. A notable convert to Lope Martin's cause was Juan de Zaldivar, the scribe, who had access to Pericon's writings and plans.

It was not yet too late for Pericon to suppress the trouble, however, and that was what Garnica the constable, Fray Juan de Viveros the chaplain, and the loyal Martinez pressed him to do. The plotters, so far as numbers went, formed only a small minority of the ship's company, and the rank and file of the soldiery could be expected to obey the captain's orders. Furthermore Rodrigo del Angle, the bo'sun, knew a little about navigation and said he was confident he could take the ship to Zebu if Lope Martin were displaced from his position as pilot.

Captain Pericon turned a deaf ear to the appeals of the loyalists. He was not disposed to turn over the ship to the inexperienced Angle, nor take the extreme step of restraining Martin, Mosquera and Solorzano by force. This was less because he hesitated to visit violence on his men than because of an innate infatuation and a contempt for the advice of others.

On 30 May Bartolomé de Lara, who with Campo was Martin's intimate, tackled the ensign about the lack of food and drink. He said that he and the other sailors had to work hard in all weathers, and the rations were inadequate for them.

Young Pericon's reply was contemptuous, and seizing a spike he struck at Lara with it. Lara drew his dagger from his belt and made for the ensign, who set up a great hubbub and went down to get his sword, appearing soon after on deck with some soldiers armed with muskets.

By this time Lara had taken refuge in the rigging.

Pilot Martin, observing all this, tried to make the helmsman understand that when the ensign and the soldiers were

in the low waist of the ship he should put the helm hard
over so as to throw them overboard. This risk was ever-
present on the *San Jeronimo* even without intention, since
owing to Lope Martin's haste to get away from Acapulco
before Nemesis caught up with him there was insufficient
ballast in the ship. But the trick failed because the helmsman
did not get the idea quickly enough, although everything was
in confusion for a time as the ship heeled.

The ensign now held the upper hand. He ordered Lara to
come down on pain of being shot down if he did not. Lara
came down and was confined below decks.

The rebels armed themselves forthwith. In this they were
aided by the fact that the quartermaster, Alonso Alvarez, a
mulatto, was another of Lope Martin's followers. Some arms
were also provided by Juan de Zaldivar, the scribe.

These goings-on were reported to Captain Pericon by
Martinez and the chaplain. They prayed him to suppress the
conspirators before it was too late. Pericon, with a derisive
smile, answered that he was not afraid of the rabble and
would hang anybody who got out of hand.

This, noted Martinez sadly, was typical of Captain
Pericon. He did nothing to deserve the loyalty of his soldiers,
treating them like servants, and never discussing things
with them.

The three-day Festival of the Ascension now commenced,
but it was a time of ominous foreboding and not of joy. The
weather was fitful, with leaden skies and seas and sweltering
heat interspersed with rain and fog.

On 3 June, 1566, which was the second day of the Festival
and a good occasion for a surprise, the plotters were ready.
They met on the poop. Chief Sergeant Mosquera, having
been deluded into thinking the Pericons had evil intentions
against himself as well as the other plotters, had rather less
unworthy motives than the rest. He was therefore the

perfect Brutus for the actual killing of the Pericons. He and
Lara, it was agreed, would assassinate Pericon like a petty
Caesar in his cabin below the poop, and his son with him.
The violent Lara would have the added taste of revenge on
young Pericon in doing so. Two soldiers who were in the
plot, Alonso Vaca and Alonso Zarfate, would go along with
them as supporters. Lope Martin and the others would see
to it that the attention of the rest of the soldiers and the
ship's company was distracted and that the guards were kept
in their quarters.

The conspirators divided their forces accordingly and
went about their work.

Now there happened to be a trap-door from above giving
access to a passage close to the door of the cabin occupied by
Pericon and his son. Nothing could have been better for
Mosquera's and Lara's part of the plan. They let themselves
stealthily through the trap-door, followed by Vaca and
Zarfate. Meanwhile Lope Martin and the others, swords in
hands, went below.

Mosquera and Lara burst in to the captain's cabin. They
plunged their daggers into Pericon and his son, so that they
died a cruel and bitter death. As a macabre sequel, Zarfate
wiped the blood from the daggers on a stocking and a sleeve
in order to make trophies of them to the glorification of the
assassins.

Meanwhile, in the narrow congested quarters where the
soldiers were sleeping, some of them perceived that something was afoot. Lope Martin then told them to stay where
they were, as it was nothing, and to show they meant business
he and his companions brandished their swords.

When the deed was done Mosquera went forth saying
that the treacherous dogs, the Pericons, had thought to
murder him and his friends the sailors.

Mosquera immediately issued an order that all arms

would have to be given up forthwith on pain of death, and
Sergeant Solorzano had them collected under lock and key.

The next morning the ship's company met to elect a new
captain. Few tears were dropped for the Pericons. Mosquera,
indeed, gave an air of virtue to the crime.

A corporal of the soldiery proposed the name of Chief
Sergeant Mosquera. Mosquera, continuing his role of
Brutus, said that he was pleased that they should understand
his motives in removing the Pericons, but there were
worthier men than he to be captain, and if such a man were
elected he would willingly obey him.

The majority, however, pressed Mosquera to accept, and
he finally acceded. He asked that they should not call him
captain, but only chief sergeant as theretofore. He said that
he would lead them to Captain-General Legazpi, who would
understand why they had had to kill the Pericons to preserve
themselves.

Great consternation was felt by Lope Martin and Campo
at this turn of events. As Cassius to Mosquera's Brutus,
Campo had egged Mosquera on, poisoned his mind against
Captain Pericon, and fed his contempt and envy for the
young and callow ensign. But now Mosquera was leader,
and proposing to take them to Zebu, where their lives would
not be worth anything in face of an inquiry.

Martin and Campo and their fellow-conspirators therefore
now had all the more incentive to get control of the ship,
load it with spices and gold in the Isles of the West, and sail
to somewhere outside the Spanish domains. They decided
to bide their time, dissembling their thoughts in the meantime.

Meanwhile Mosquera was not doing a bad job as leader.
He went out of his way to conciliate the people on the ship
and treat them well, which was a great change after the
Pericons.

In due course Mosquera decided to try a little intrigue on his own account against Lope Martin. He knew that Bo'sun Angle had told Pericon that he thought he could get the ship to Zebu. Mosquera therefore approached Angle with a proposal that he should be pilot in place of Lope Martin, Mosquera's thought being to execute Martin as an incorrigible trouble-maker. Mosquera found Angle was agreeable. Mosquera then approached four soldiers who had supported him in his intention of going to Legazpi at Zebu. Their names were Marcos de Cubillas, Antonio de Cucarella, Miguel de Luarca and Alberto de Horozco. The four agreed to co-operate, the proposal being that they should be armed in preparation for the execution of Martin. Such a plan required both resolution and cunning. Mosquera, however, was no match for Lope Martin and Campo when it came to intrigue. It was not long before the latter had a good idea of Mosquera's intentions. Furthermore Sergeant Solorzano had thrown in his lot with Martin and Campo.

On 21 June, Lope Martin's faction were ready to forestall Mosquera. When night fell they went about their several commissions.

First the soldiers Vaca and Zarfate – the very two who had supported Mosquera when he killed the Pericons in their cabin – held Mosquera in talk in his quarters in the forecastle, while Sergeant Solorzano and some of the others went down to where the soldiers were sleeping.

Solorzano, when the soldiers roused, told them that his orders were to collect their arms immediately, and that anyone who resisted would be shot.

The arms of the people who were not in the plot were thus seized and put under lock and key, with the result that the conspirators against Mosquera had control of the ship. Angle and the four soldiers who had conspired with Mosquera against Martin were held prisoners under strong

suspicion, although Martin did not know precisely what had
been afoot between them.

At one time when all this was going on, Mosquera's
attention was attracted by the noise. He proposed that they
should go and see what it was about. Mosquera had already
started on his way down to the soldiers' quarters, but Vaca
and Zarfate called him back, saying that it was nothing. The
whole night was thus passed in talk. After a time Lope
Martin and some of the others joined them, and they all ate
salt pork and drank wine, with much cheerful conversation.

As if to play a practical joke on Mosquera, some of his
false friends suddenly snapped some shackles on his feet.
All of them had a good laugh at this, including Mosquera.
Then they took him out on deck and tied his arms and seated
him on a chest alongside a rope slung over a yard-arm, as if
to put him on trial.

Mosquera still remained deluded, thinking that Vaca and
Zarfate were his friends, and not realizing they were in
league with Lope Martin against him. He laughed and said,
'What foolery is this?'

To this Martin replied, 'Confess before you die.'

Mosquera, still smiling, asked why.

'Because you killed the captain and wanted to kill me,'
replied Martin.

Mosquera suddenly realized it was no game they were
playing.

At this stage the chaplain came forward and protested in
shocked alarm. But Lope Martin turned his back on the
friar even while he was talking.

This was a signal to the sailors who were standing by the
rope to put the noose round the neck of the helpless
Mosquera and hoist him on high, without time to confess.
Then they let him down, and tossed him, still in his shackles,
and still half alive, into the sea.

8

Jetsam on Ujelang

AFTER Mosquera had followed the Pericons to a watery grave, Lope Martin, with Campo as his adviser, was top dog of the *San Jeronimo*. No pretence was made of an election. The mutineers had control of the arms, and nobody else on board could argue with them. Martin and his cabal followed a secretive policy about their intentions, but it was known that they were pursuing Lope Martin's cherished project of making for the Isles of the West or Japan to get a load of spices by fair means or foul. Since they had few trade goods on board, it was plain that the means that would in fact be open to them would be foul, and that from the time Mosquera's plan to join Legazpi in Zebu went overboard with Mosquera himself, the *San Jeronimo* was to all intents and purposes a pirate ship.

Lope Martin's emergence as the dictator of their immediate destinies brought fear to the hearts of the core of loyalists who had tried to stand by Captain Pericon. Santiago de Garnica, the constable, who had tried to warn Pericon, Rodrigo del Angle, who had been willing to displace Lope Martin as pilot, and the four soldiers who had been willing to co-operate with Mosquera in executing Martin, now lived in fear of their lives. It was only because the mutineers had no firm information against them and in any case intended to put ashore in due course all who were not prepared to throw in their lot with them, that these suspects were being spared.

After a time the strain began to tell on the nerves of Rodrigo del Angle, the bo'sun. He secretly asked Molina, the steward, an old shipmate who had joined Martin's faction, to intercede on his behalf with Martin, saying he would be willing to go off with Martin on his intended enterprises, whatever they might be. Martin needed all the skilled assistance he could get in working the ship. For the time being he chose to keep Angle guessing, waging a war of nerves on him.

Lope Martin knew they must now be nearing the Marshalls – called Los Barbudos from Legazpi's name for the fertile and friendly Mejit. Lope himself had passed through the Marshalls the previous year in the *San Lucas*. Each night the ship's boat went ahead, scouting for the land. The hopes of the whole ship's company were buoyed up with the thought of being on land again after nearly two months at sea.

On Sunday, 29 June, 1566, the lookout shouted that land was ahead. The people on board gazed out eagerly, but as the ship drew near, all they saw was a low atoll consisting of about seventeen islets strung together with reefs in a circle like a rosary, with no sign of habitation.

Lope Martin decided to push on to the west, saying that there were better islands ahead, and that they still had some of the Acapulco water left.

The next evening they came to another atoll made up of many islets. A canoe with eight islanders in it came out and stopped at a distance from the ship. The people in it gazed wonderingly at the strange visitant for a time, and then, as night fell, returned to the land. Next morning the last of the islets was searched for water by a landing-party, but all they found were the footprints of the islanders who occasionally visited it. A great plague of flies bothered the people on the ship at this island.

The following day the *San Jeronimo* came to another low

atoll. As the ship came close to its western part, they had an agreeable surprise. On a beach they saw a pleasant little settlement among the palms, with a small gathering of the inhabitants. A small canoe with the local chief and a follower came off to the ship, and after receiving some gifts the chief went back to the island in a very good temper. The way was thereby opened up for a peaceful landing, and the ship's boat plied back and forth taking parties of the visitors ashore. The women of the settlement proved to be darkly beautiful, and received the visitors with the beating of drums, singing and dancing. Five barrels of water were brought on board, as well as coconuts, plantains and yams, and pearl-shell fish-hooks as souvenirs. In return the visitors gave 'trivial gifts'.

Two years later the Spanish explorer Alvaro de Mendaña, having crossed the Pacific from Peru to his epic discovery of the Solomons, came up into the Marshalls while making his way back to America. At an island which was certainly Namu, since Mendaña's account describes it in unmistakable detail, a landing-party found a nail made into the form of a small file or chisel, and also some European rope. Perhaps these were some of the 'trivial gifts' given by the people of the *San Jeronimo* to the friendly islanders two years before.

The same evening the *San Jeronimo* set sail again. Martin and his associates had decided to make for Guam. They therefore changed course to the north-west in order to come up from the ninth parallel of latitude to the thirteenth, whereupon their intention was to run west to Guam.

After the ship had gone about a hundred leagues from the friendly island and was in latitude $9\frac{2}{3}$ degrees north, they were sailing at night without keeping a proper lookout when suddenly they found themselves confronted with land. They were almost surrounded by islands and rocks, toward which the current was sweeping the ship.

Lope Martin and Lara then heard the helmsman call out asking whether he should put the ship on shore. It seemed better to go ashore on land rather than court complete disaster on the reefs.

The pilot called to the helmsman to do no such thing. Lara rushed at the helmsman with curses, thrusting the man bodily aside.

Lara swung the helm this way and that, while the ship grazed the reefs. Suddenly a narrow channel only a good stone's throw wide appeared. They ran through it into completely calm water beyond. Here they dropped anchor, getting good bottom near an island.

In the morning they found themselves in a great lagoon several leagues across, with many islets and reefs enclosing it. The water of the lagoon was limpid and still. The palms on the larger islets of the atoll gave them a pleasant and refreshing appearance.

This was Ujelang, the westernmost island in the Marshalls. It is one of the most isolated islands in the Marshalls, which are themselves among the most isolated in the world.

Martin and Lara, by nerve, skill and luck, had performed the remarkable feat of taking the *San Jeronimo* at night through the narrow passage in the south side of Ujelang into the lagoon. The lagoon has only one other entrance, a wide passage somewhat to the west of the smaller one.

The *San Jeronimo* was now anchored close to a flat, fertile, attractive-looking island with about three hundred palm trees. On it were four unoccupied huts. There was a well or natural pond of water, from which the people of the *San Jeronimo* were able to quench their thirst without stint. They also had plenty of coconuts, the milk and flesh of which tasted sweet after their short rations of mouldy sour biscuit.

Lope Martin and his intimates now held a council. They discussed what to do with the loyalists and others who could not be trusted to go along with them on their piratical enterprises. Campo was all for leaving them on Ujelang. Lope Martin was inclined to leave the decision until they got to Guam or even the Philippines. Campo's sterner view, however, prevailed.

The mutineers now set about sounding out secretly and individually the uncompromised members of the ship's company. They made glittering promises to the waverers, saying that they would all be rich men from the gold and other loot they would get. This meant that no man could be sure where the others stood.

Orders were now issued that the soldiers and their gear must be shifted ashore so that repairs could be made to the ship. It was suspected, with good reason, that this was a pretext to make it easier to leave behind those who were not wanted. But no resistance was possible, since the arms were locked up on the ship apart from a dozen or so in the hands of the ringleaders and their trusted followers.

One day three sailing canoes were seen coming across the lagoon from one of the islets at a distance. They had round sails, with an outrigger as a balancer. Two of the canoes approached the island close to the ships, while the third, which contained women and children, stood off a little.

Martin, who was on the ship with the sailors, got into the ship's boat with some armed supporters, and told the rowers to make for the canoes as fast as possible. Meanwhile Sergeant Solorzano on shore had taken cover with some soldiers in some thickets near the beach, thinking to seize the canoes and their inhabitants as they disembarked. Just as the canoes touched the beach, the occupants, taking fright at the approach of the ship's boat, sailed off again. The soldiers on shore then dashed into the shallows, but the canoes were much too fast for them, and soon were miles away across the lagoon.

E

At this fiasco Lope Martin was much put out. He said he wanted to make the islanders fish for the Europeans while they were at the island, and make the women serve them.

So taken up was Lope with the idea of making serfs of the islanders that next day he took a party in the ship's boat and went to the place across the lagoon from which the canoes had come. But all he found were some deserted huts which had been abandoned so hurriedly that a sailing canoe, the construction of which was almost complete, had been left behind. It was big enough to hold thirty men.

After Lope returned, he discussed the presence of the sailing canoe at the other islet with Campo and his other cronies. They decided to go and bring it back in due course in order to use it to scatter the people on shore over the other islets. They intended to gull the soldiers by saying that this would ease the food situation while they were at the island, but their real motive was to make it easier to sail off and leave them behind. Martin spread the word around that they would stay at Ujelang over the winter, in order to conceal their real intentions.

Lope Martin was now so pleased with himself that he began to fancy himself as a new Cortes. His ideas of becoming a gentleman adventurer were, thought Martinez, much above his station.

One day Lope came ashore and addressed a cautionary tale to the assembled soldiers. He said that some time previously he had landed at Vera Cruz on the east coast of Mexico after bringing some ships there from Cuba. He told his crews he was going off into the inland parts of Mexico to seek a fortune, saying there would be good pickings for those who came with him, but that those who wanted to go back to Cuba in the ships would be at liberty to do so. They accordingly expressed their preferences, so that Lope knew those who would be co-operative. He then gave the others the rough edge of his tongue, saying that they would be made by the willing ones and himself to come with them, and he would make them suffer for wanting to hold out on him. This, said Lope, had accordingly happened, and he went off with the sheep and the goats after burning the ships.

This, felt Martinez, was a cunning exercise in psychological torture on Lope Martin's part, calculated to make more soldiers rally to him in his project of becoming a new *conquistador*.

Martinez's sense of isolation and danger was increased when he found that his close friend among the soldiers, Rodrigo de la Cervilla, had succumbed to the blandishments bestowed on him, and had thrown in his lot with the mutineers.

Lope Martin, as it was found out later, dramatized his piratical intentions by telling those who decided to go with him that they must swear before a consecrated host to die rather than retreat, and to renounce their fatherlands.

While nobody could be sure just who were or who were not on Lope Martin's side, there were some who were plainly in bad odour with the mutineers. One of these was Rodrigo del Angle, the bo'sun, who was rightly suspected by Martin and his supporters of having been willing to pilot the ship to Zebu in place of Martin. Angle had tried secretly to treat with the mutineers, but they were keeping him on tenterhooks. Another who was in jeopardy was the constable, Santiago de Garnica, who was suspected of having warned Pericon against the plotters, and who lived in fear of his life.

Most astonishing, however, was the fact that after the ship had been some time at Ujelang Bartolomé de Lara, the assassin of the Pericons and erstwhile close crony of Martin, had fallen out with his new master. Some quarrel had taken place between them, as often happens between associates of Martin's and Lara's lawless temperament. As a result the moody Lara took to sulking on the ship, scarcely ever going ashore, and even on occasion giving way to tears.

Juan Martinez, the conscientious old soldier, who was himself regarded with no enthusiasm by the rebels, was one day engaged in furtive conversation by Bo'sun Angle. Angle said that he and Garnica had discussed the possibility of making off with the ship. They had it in mind to approach Lara, since he was no longer friendly with Martin. Angle asked Martinez if he thought he could get some of the soldiers to support them.

Martinez agreed to sound out some of the soldiers, although he knew he was taking his life in his hands in approaching them. First he took a trusted friend named San Juan de Goyri into his confidence. Between them they persuaded about half a dozen soldiers whom they could rely on.

Meanwhile Angle and Garnica had made their play with Lara on the ship. The bait they offered him was that if he would throw in his lot with them, they would make him captain.

Lara's mood changed rapidly at this improvement in his prospects. If the plan came off he would be top dog, and no longer at Martin's mercy. He therefore accepted. This helped to get others of the crew on their side. One was Morales, a former conspirator with Martin but a close friend of Lara.

Their most useful recruit was Juan de Enrique, a gunner. He had the great advantage of being admired by Lope Martin himself, and was privy to his plans.

On shore Martinez took the chaplain, Fray Juan de Viveros, into his confidence. The soldiers who had pledged themselves to Martinez were then powerfully confirmed in their good intentions by the chaplain. During confession he reached their hearts by exhorting them to do their duty to God, King and country.

Martinez and the other soldiers in the counter-plot were

confined to the island, with no good pretext for going on board the ship. They could not defy Solorzano, Campo and their armed associates on shore. Prospects of getting out to the ship when the counter-plotters decided to strike, therefore, depended on their being picked up at night clandestinely by their confederates on the ship in the ship's boat.

Lope Martin and his intimates, knowing nothing of the threat to their own plans, now decided to proceed with their intention to divide the people on shore among the other islets surrounding the lagoon. In order to facilitate this they decided to go and fetch the native canoe which Lope Martin had found at the deserted village across the lagoon.

When Lara, Angle and Garnica heard of this from Enrique, it caused them considerable alarm. Their plan to steal the *San Jeronimo* would be jeopardized so long as the ship's boat was away, and when the sailing canoe had been brought to the anchorage it would be so much more difficult to deny Martin and his supporters access to the ship. They decided they must make their coup without further delay, since time was running out.

The next day, 16 July, was destined to be the occasion of high drama.

First Enrique managed to persuade Martin not to send the boat away that day to the islet across the lagoon to fetch the sailing canoe, saying that there was much to do and that the boat was needed.

Shortly thereafter Lope Martin and some of his sailors were taking the altitude of the sun. On the island the chaplain was celebrating Mass. Suddenly Martin, having had some difference with the sailors, started to shout curses and blasphemies. One of his verbal sallies, directed at the celebrants on shore, was, 'Shackling yourselves to God won't get you any gain.'

Now it happened that the scribe, Juan de Zaldivar, who

had been an accomplice of Martin in the mutiny but had
been put in irons on the ship for some reason, was at this
very moment being released. As his irons were struck off, the
noise of the clash of metal carried plainly to the shore,
accompanied by Lope's storming and shouting.

This gave the impression to Martinez and his counter-
plotters on shore that Lara and the rest on the ship must
have been found out, and caused them much consternation.
It was found afterwards that one of Martinez's accomplices
had considered making a confession of the counter-conspiracy
on the spot, in the hope of saving their lives.

Soon afterwards the ship's boat came ashore with Martin,
Angle and Garnica. Martinez saw with relief that the plot had
not been discovered. The news that Angle gave Martinez
when they got a few minutes alone was not, however, reassuring. Angle said that he and Lara and Garnica would have
liked to make their attempt on the ship the previous night,
that they had had another cause for alarm that morning when
Lope Martin had been persuaded by Enrique not to send the
boat away until the next day, and that they must act without
delay.

When Martinez pointed out that he and his supporters
could not hope to get out to the ship before that night,
Angle, whose nerves were very much on edge, answered
that it was beginning to look very much as if Martinez and
his friends would get him executed.

Martinez sought out his friend Goyri, and found that in
the meantime he had been having a talk with Garnica. Garnica
had agreed with Goyri that the plan to seize the ship should
be applied that night.

Angle, however, had other ideas. Summoning Garnica,
Angle got into the boat with Garnica and bade the crew
take them immediately to the ship. There Lara and Enrique
were awaiting them. In few words it was agreed that they
should move to save their own skins forthwith.

The four of them rushed down below and armed themselves with swords. Led by Lara and Enrique who were noted for their fighting ability, the swordsmen came up on deck making passes with their weapons, striking sparks with them, and generally playing the part of Mars. They showed they meant business by attacking the astonished quartermaster, Alonso Alvarez. Alvarez, having received a swordcut, incontinently leapt into the sea and swam ashore where he conveyed the news of the counter-revolt to Martin, Campo and the others.

Martin at first refused to believe that he had been tricked, saying that the people on board must be drunk. Shortly thereafter, however, the fact that Lara had turned against his former associates was made plain by Lara himself. He came to the side of the ship and called to Campo, who had been his close friend. He said that he would accept Campo for the sake of friendship if he came out to the ship. This offer Campo refused, saying he would come out to the ship indeed, but with the intention of dealing with Lara and the dogs who had joined him.

Martin and Campo were still confident that they and their friends on the ship would get the better of Lara and his followers.

Meanwhile Lara, Garnica, Enrique, Angle, Morales and their supporters on the ship had in fact succeeded in subduing all opposition. It proved to be easy, for Martin's allies on the ship for the most part behaved like rats.

Juan de Zaldivar, the scribe, having first been in and then out of the good books of the mutineers, and then forgiven by them to the extent of being released from his shackles only that morning, now found himself out of luck again. His new masters showed their contempt for him by giving him a cut with a sword, so that he jumped overboard. He then pleaded with them from the water, saying that if they received him back he would be a faithful servant of the King.

He was then allowed to come back on board. As things
turned out, it might have been better for him if he had swum
ashore.

One unfortunate incident took place when a lad who had
the key of the armoury could not find it quickly enough to
please the nervous and impatient Angle. Angle hit the youth
cruelly on the head with his sword, but fortunately the
wound healed well.

All those on board who were not known to be positive
supporters of Lara and his associates were disarmed, and the
latter thus had control of the ship.

Meanwhile Martin and Campo were urging their followers
on shore to swim out to the ship. They bade some try to
board the ship, and others to seize the boat at the ship's side.

Some of the sailors on shore dashed into the sea and
started to swim the short distance to the ship. They were not,
however, the only ones to take to the water, for the soldiers
Cubillas and Cucarella, two of the erstwhile supporters of
Mosquera who were out of Martin's good books, jumped into
the sea and swam out to the ship also. Two other soldiers
who had not sided with Martin followed them. When the
sailors of Martin's persuasion got out to the ship, they were
promptly seized and confined below decks. Enrique had got
into the ship's boat to make sure that nobody from the shore
or the ship could get possession of it. Cubillas, Cucarella and
the other two soldiers who had swum out were given arms.

When these things were accomplished, Bo'sun Angle set
about putting as much distance as possible as quickly as
possible between the redoubtable Martin and the ship, even
if it meant the abandonment of friends as well as foes. He
could not even wait to haul up the anchors, but cut the two
cables and set sail. Nor did he have any instruments or charts,
which were on shore, together with the maintopsail and
main bonnet.

With sinking hearts Martinez and the chaplain and the loyal soldiers, and no less the mutineers themselves, watched the ship make slowly for the passage through which it had entered the lagoon. But the ship had to return, for there was little wind and the current was contrary, so that the ship could not make any way. Since its new commanders dared not anchor close to the island where the camp was, they pulled out into the lagoon to a point about a mile away.

The hard core of the mutineers on shore now numbered Lope Martin, Campo, Solorzano, Vaca, Zarfate, Molina, Alvarez and a few other hangers-on. They were greatly outnumbered by the rest of the soldiers, but the latter had no arms, whereas the mutineers had a dozen muskets. Nevertheless the mutineers could not afford to relax their vigilance.

Martin, Campo and their cronies now had a conference. They decided to send out three soldiers as envoys to the ship on a raft of logs and barrels, with instructions to offer the navigation instruments and charts in return for food. The raft proved unmanageable and drifted with the currents.

Meanwhile Lara, being still hopeful of persuading Campo and others of his erstwhile shipmates to come away with him, came towards the shore in the ship's boat, intending to hail the camp from a safe distance off shore. The two soldiers who had followed Cubillas and Cucarella into the water to the ship earlier in the day were with Lara, armed with muskets.

Now it happened that one of the three soldiers on the raft was one Pero Martinez de Estadela, against whom Lara had some grudge. When Lara approached the raft in the ship's boat and saw that Estadela was on it, Lara ordered his musketeers to shoot Estadela in cold blood. Not content with this, when the boat came up with the raft, Lara struck Estadela a cruel blow with his sword. Estadela fell into the sea, and died a bitter death with the salt water paining his wounds.

The other men on the raft managed to get to a small island near the camp, and so back to Martin.

Lara then came cautiously within hailing distance of the shore. As the boat approached, the mutineers ordered the chaplain and soldiers to withdraw to the distance of a musket-shot from the beach and sit down.

Martin, being never one to lose an opportunity for a bit of over-statement, called out to the boat that they had killed two of the three envoys on the raft, and that the other looked in a bad way too.

Lara then said that any of the people on shore who wanted to come to the ship must do so at once. Campo and the other mutineers, however, were too shrewd to entrust themselves to the mercy of the loyalists on board – a calculation which was wise in the light of later events. Nor would Campo hear of the release of the chaplain or any of the soldiers, threatening to shoot any who tried to make for the beach. Lara therefore returned to the ship without any of the people on shore.

Now from their new station farther out in the lagoon, the people on the ship could see what appeared to be a second channel out of the lagoon, to the west of the narrow one by which they had entered. This was in fact the wider passage through the Ujelang reef.

When therefore Lara got back to the ship, Angle proposed that they sail immediately for this passage. Lara, however, was still possessed of some doubts, coupled with some senti-ment towards his late associates. He said he thought that on the way out they should leave on a small islet which lay to port some wine for Mass, and some beans and maize for planting, so that the people who were left on shore could find them.

Lara accordingly went in the ship's boat with three or four men toward the islet, while the ship picked its way across the lagoon. It happened that there were some reefs and rocks in the way that the ship was going, so that it got into considerable danger. Angle and Garnica, not liking this, called out to Lara that the ship was in danger of going aground and that it would be wise for him to come back at once. But Lara continued on to the islet, shouting back: 'If we get stuck we'll just have to go ashore for fifty men.'

This dark saying struck a cold chill into the hearts of Angle and Garnica. They thought their moody associate might go off to the camp in the ship's boat. But fortunately the ship got clear of the danger, and Lara, having put the wine and seeds on shore, returned to the ship.

Since night was coming on, and they could not see to navigate, they were obliged to drop anchor in the lagoon. The point where they did so was about four miles from the camp.

As the people on ship and shore settled down for the night, their minds and hearts were ill at ease.

In the morning the mutineers, thinking the ship might come back to attack them, put everybody to work cutting palms and making a protective palisade.

After a while the ship's boat was seen approaching. In it were Lara, Garnica and Enrique. The new commanders of the ship had thought better of going off without the charts and instruments, and were disposed to parley. They shouted out to the people on shore that they would give food if the instruments were sent out to them.

At this point Martinez decided that he would appeal openly to the mutineers to send somebody who would be acceptable as an envoy. Martinez had a few tense moments when Lope Martin drew him aside. It seemed to the watching soldiers that Martinez's last moment had come. But Martin merely gave Martinez a lot of talk about what to say to the people on the ship. Martinez then waded into the sea with a log to support him, and managed to get to the waiting boat.

Lara now said that they would go back to the ship and sail

without delay, as Angle wanted them to do. Martinez was much alarmed at this. He pleaded with Lara to persevere in the attempt to persuade Martin and Campo to let the loyal men on shore go. Finally a dozen sick and useless men, taking a compass, were allowed by the mutineers to go from the camp to a point where they were picked up by the boat, the understanding being that some food should be brought in return. The boat then returned to the ship.

That afternoon Garnica went with the ship's boat to the west to prospect the apparent passage through the reef. The boat was away the whole afternoon. When it returned, Garnica brought the glad news that there was a wide, easily navigable passage out of the lagoon.

While Garnica was away, the people on the ship were amazed to see two men swimming towards the ship. They were Miguel de Luarca and another soldier named Melchior Villanueva, who, having escaped from the camp, had performed the remarkable feat of swimming the four miles to the ship, resting for a while on the intermediate islet where Lara had left the wine and seeds.

Luarca's and Villanueva's escape, following on that of the four soldiers the previous day, caused some dejection to Martin and his faction. It was indeed evident that they had nothing to gain, and perhaps something to lose, by further intransigence. They decided therefore to hold six servant-lads but give the rest of the men on shore the run of the island.

This opened up the way to the rescue of most of the soldiers by the ship's boat. Martin's faction were bidden by the rescuers to withdraw to a safe distance, which they did. Extreme precautions were taken by the landing-parties to see that they were not surprised. The two sails on land and an assortment of instruments and charts were taken to the ship, but great quantities of gear and personal effects had to be left behind, including most of the soldiers' chests.

Great was the joy on the ship when the chaplain and the loyal soldiers came on board. Martinez's satisfaction was, however, marred by one cloud. Juan Jañiz, the Portuguese sailor who was Martin's friend from *San Lucas* days, had been given leave to go ashore on the last day. When Jañiz talked with Martin, he decided to share his fate. This demonstration of loyalty was somewhat marred by the fact that Jañiz, at Lope's instigation, told Martinez's friend Rodrigo de la Cervilla quite falsely that Martinez had betrayed him, and that if Cervilla returned to the ship he would be killed as a follower of Martin. This was told to Martinez by some of the last people to be rescued. They said that Cervilla had been greatly upset, going round saying that Martinez was a false friend, and refusing even to go near the boat despite the reassuring messages that were conveyed to him.

Not all the people who were left behind on Ujelang were supporters of Martin. In addition to the six servant-lads, a few loyal men were left because the nerve and patience of Angle and his associates fell short of the final test.

The final news that was brought of the mutineers and their enforced companions was when the last boat-load to leave the shore looked back and saw some people on the beach dressed in white and holding a flag. The meaning of this was obscure, there being some conjecture that it might signify that Martin himself had been killed and the remainder wished to parley. But the new masters of the *San Jeronimo*, despite Martinez's entreaties, would not suffer any further inquiry or delay. There seems no reason to think that the conjecture that Martin had been killed was anything more than a wishful surmise.

At dawn on 21 July, 1566, fifteen days after she had entered it, the *San Jeronimo* sailed out of the Ujelang lagoon into the open sea. Behind her remained twenty-seven marooned men and boys.

9

Perilous Seas & Islands

BEFORE following the company of the *San Jeronimo* on their further remarkable adventures, the intriguing question of what happened to the twenty-seven men and youths who remained on Ujelang is worth some thought. These exiles just dropped out of history and nothing was ever heard of them again. We do, however, have some clues on which to base some surmises.

The list of those who were left behind on Ujelang was recorded by Juan Martinez. It is full of silent pathos in reference to the six serving-lads who were held by force, being tied up by the mutineers so that they would not escape to the ship. Some of them were known only by a Christian name. Here are the names of the six boys: Alonso, the captain's boy; Francisco, the sergeant's boy; Francisco, the half-breed boy of Felipe del Campo; Francisco Hermoso and Francisco Montero, two cabin-boys; and Juanico, a ship's boy.

One matter of interest is whether any natives still remained on the atoll to be caught and enslaved by the mutineers. It is probable that there were not. No signs of fires or fisherfolk were noted after Martin had pursued the three sailing canoes across the lagoon, only to find the islanders had deserted their little settlement, leaving only an incomplete canoe. Legazpi the previous year had passed close to Ujelang and thought it uninhabited. It seems likely that the two or three families who had occupied the settlement when the *San Jeronimo* arrived were all the people who were on the atoll, and that they wisely chose to take their chance of perishing at sea rather than remain at the mercy of the violent men who had invaded their little Eden.

The next question that excites the imagination is whether some of the marooned men could have got away from Ujelang to other islands in the native canoe left behind by the islanders.

There was some incentive to the mutineers to go off to other islands where they might be free of the risk of being found by some later Spanish ship which might come upon their retreat either by accident or intent. But where might they hope to find such islands? The nearest island to Ujelang is Eniwetok, some 150 miles to the north-east. None of the Europeans who were left on Ujelang, however, knew of its existence, and since it is just a small dot of land in a vast expanse of sea, Eniwetok, we may safely conclude, was spared from a visitation. A possible target which was known to some of the mutineers was Guam, which was the island for which the *San Jeronimo* was making when Ujelang was encountered. But Guam is 1100 miles from Ujelang, and the *San Jeronimo* took fifteen days to get there. Guam was also on the route to the Philippines which later Spanish ships might be expected to follow. If some of the exiles tried to make Guam, their chances of reaching it were slim indeed, and if, having made it, they survived for long among the islanders without continuing supplies of ammunition may also be open to doubt. The broad position and direction of the main islands of the Marshalls, some 300 miles to the east of Ujelang, were known to the exiles, but again their chances of reaching them, or of surviving for long if they did, or even of attempting the voyage when the Marshalls, for all the exiles knew, might have been frequented by later

Spanish ships on their way to the Philippines, may be considered dubious. To the south-west of Ujelang were the Carolines, which were known to Lope Martin and Juan Jañiz from their traverse of the previous year in the *San Lucas*. The hair-raising encounters of the *San Lucas* with the Caroline Islanders, however, would be fresh in their minds. Again, therefore, if any of the exiles of Ujelang ever did set out for the Carolines, which is doubtful, or got there over the great expanse of ocean which lies between, which is more doubtful still, their chances of survival were small indeed.

Whatever may have been the answer to the question of whether or not all the people who were left behind on Ujelang were content to remain there, it is safe to conclude that some of them must have done so. For when water and food had been put in the canoe, as well as other necessary gear, there would certainly not have been room for all twenty-seven. Perhaps the truth is that all of them remained to live out their lives.

There is no doubt that a number of men, by living on coconuts and shell-fish and other edible materials deposited on the reefs, could have survived indefinitely. Those of the marooned men and youths who chose to remain, or had no choice but to remain, on Ujelang were not the last European adventurers to spend a period of exile there. 'Bully' Hayes, black-birder and semi-pirate in the 19th century, hid out on Ujelang for several years with some of his followers.

Just what might have happened in the way of quarrels, intrigues, contests for leadership, and exploitation of the weaker members of the rebel band and their captives when the *San Jeronimo* had left them on Ujelang is an interesting speculation. The last word on this was given by Martinez himself when he wrote: 'We shall not know until God wishes.'

Perhaps somewhere on the bottom of Ujelang lagoon, buried in the sand and coral, still lie the remains of the two anchors which were abandoned by Bo'sun Angle in his hurry to get away from Lope Martin.

Lope Martin's brief entry into the annals of the Pacific was certainly spectacular. No one can rob him of his just fame for being the first navigator in history to take a vessel from the Americas across the Pacific and back again, nor of his notoriety as one of the boldest and cunningest of mutineers.

We now leave the mutineers and their prisoners and rejoin the *San Jeronimo* as it sails out of Ujelang lagoon.

The original company of 170 on the ship when it left Acapulco had now dwindled to 136. The senior commanders were all gone. Captain Pericon, Ensign Pericon Mesa and Chief Sergeant Mosquera had been assassinated, and Sergeant Solorzano was left on Ujelang. Of the ship's officers, Pilot Lope Martin, Quartermaster Alvarez and Steward Molina were also marooned on Ujelang.

Bartolomé de Lara, a sailor, was now captain of the *San Jeronimo*. His friend Morales was steward—a not unimportant post, since it had to do with the food and water. Rodrigo del Angle, the erstwhile bo'sun, was now pilot, and the only man on board with any skill in navigation by instruments. Santiago de Garnica, the ship's constable, and Juan de Enrique, the gunner, completed the new 'brass'.

It was not long, however, before new tensions began to develop on the *San Jeronimo*. Angle showed a suspicious and intractable spirit towards his colleagues. Light on the stress which lay behind this was thrown by his admission to a shipmate that he had secretly tried to join the mutineers. He thus had the unquiet mind of a man who had evaded one threat but had not yet certainly saved himself.

The first schism that developed was between Lara and Morales on the one hand, and Angle, Garnica and Enrique on the other. It came to the ears of the latter that Lara and

Morales appeared to be conspiring together. It was said that
Lara had suggested that Lope Martin's idea of going off and
getting a load of gold and spices and taking it back to Spain
was a good one, and would even win them commendation
in the eyes of God and King alike. Two other sailors, Gorjon
and Rodriguez, were reported to be implicated in these
suggestions. Support appeared to be given to these accusations by the fact that Lara and Morales were all the time
consorting together and whispering, being aided in this by
the fact that they shared quarters.

Swiftly Angle and Garnica, who had no cause to trust
Lara after his nerve-racking changes of heart at Ujelang,
moved to seize him and his three alleged associates. Lara was
incontinently sentenced to be executed. Morales was
deprived of the stewardship. The other two were released.

Lara now suffered the fate he had helped to visit on
Mosquera. He was hanged in his shackles, and then flung
into the sea, still in the shackles.

Lara was obviously not a good intriguer, being wayward
and careless in showing his hand.

Command of the *San Jeronimo* was proving a hazardous
occupation, Pericon, Mosquera, Martin and Lara having all
come to grief in rapid succession. Yet command, if firmly
held, is sometimes a condition of survival. So apparently
thought Angle after Lara's exit from the leadership. According to the Spanish custom, the pilot of a ship was a sailing-
master, not a commander. Angle had therefore perhaps less
claim to be leader than Garnica, the ship's constable, or
Enrique, the gunner. This, however, was by no means
Angle's view of the matter. He arrogated authority to
himself. Furthermore he became very suspicious of his
colleagues, so that if they were seen even to be in conversation with each other, he would threaten them.

Angle had one trump card. He was the only navigator on

the ship. His associates therefore were constrained to let him have his way, so that they might have a chance of reaching Zebu without further trouble. But great was the tension on the *San Jeronimo*, with fear and suspicion stalking at everybody's heels.

There were still two members of Lope Martin's former faction on the ship. These were Morales, and Zaldivar, the scribe. It was not long before Morales was reported to have been saying suspicious things. He and Zaldivar and a soldier who was said to be implicated were seized and confined in irons. At the end of four days the three prisoners were brought on deck to suffer their fate. First Morales was hanged. Then Zaldivar was brought to the rope.

At this stage Juan Martinez intervened. He said he had no brief for Zaldivar, but it was the King's law that he should have a proper trial. That could only be given when they reached Zebu, for none on the ship had the authority.

This statement shook the confidence of Zaldivar's would-be executioners. It could not be said that a mere scribbler offered any dire threat. So Zaldivar and the soldier were reprieved and put back in prison.

On 4 August Rota, the island of the Marianas immediately north of Guam, came in sight. The inexperienced Angle had at least not missed the Marianas.

Angle told the crew of the ship's boat to coast the north of the island while he took the ship round the south side.

After the boat's crew had gone off with some soldiers to support them, the *San Jeronimo* came round to the south-west or lee side of Rota, which proved to be a fine fertile island with attractive plantations, and very populous. Great numbers of canoes put off from the island, offering fish, coconuts, fruit and water. Although the *San Jeronimo* was the first European ship to touch at Rota, the islanders showed they knew of iron, Guam and Rota being in close contact.

The company of the *San Jeronimo* thronged the deck to see the island and the canoes, thereby causing the ship to cant dangerously because of the lack of ballast. The temperamental Angle got quite beside himself with rage over this.

Some of the soldiers were by no means averse from having a bit of target practice at the expense of the people in the canoes. Their shots caused consternation among the islanders, numbers of whom jumped into the water. Again Martinez interceded in the name of humanity, and the shooting was stopped.

On the west side of the island Angle found a good anchorage, where they were rejoined by the ship's boat. Near the anchorage there was a fine beach, with many huts set in the palms.

The next day, while Angle and some others stayed on the ship as guards, most of the ship's company went ashore. Although the people received them without arms, again offering fruit, coconuts and fish, some of the undisciplined mob of soldiers got out of hand and killed half a dozen or more of the villagers. This provoked the defenders to try to seek vengeance. During the two and a half days that the *San Jeronimo* was at Rota, more than two hundred of the villagers' houses were destroyed and more people were killed.

After this interlude at Rota, the *San Jeronimo* set sail for the Philippines.

During the next week or so, good progress was made with a following wind from the north-east. Not so satisfactory, however, was the state of affairs on the ship itself. The suspicious Angle got more and more difficult. He had insisted that the generality be disarmed, and showed a disposition to arrest and threaten with death anybody on whom his suspicions fell.

Further anxieties were caused by the inevitable pessimists.

'How do we know we will ever get to Zebu?' they would ask. 'And how do we know that Captain-General Legazpi will be there if we do?' These questions were indeed not entirely idle, since Pilot Angle was in unfamiliar waters, and it was in any case nearly a year since the last word of Legazpi had been conveyed.

After seven days of good sailing from the Marianas, the people of the *San Jeronimo* estimated that they could not be very far from the Philippines. Then a tremendous storm struck them. Not only did it strike terror into the soldiers who were unused to the sea, but the sailors also said they had seen nothing like it. It brought down the topmasts and broke the mizzen and some of the spars. The ship could make no progress, and neither could the birds overhead, many of them falling exhausted on the *San Jeronimo*'s decks.

The truth of the matter was that they had come into the zone of the south-west monsoon, which blows in the winter months, often with great violence, between the Philippines and the Marianas.

For thirty long days the *San Jeronimo* struggled against the adverse winds. The ship's company prayed to San Lorenzo for deliverance, and contributed to a charity in his name. But for their sins they were forced slowly back until the peaks of Guam itself came in sight.

Angle, thinking to make a landing in a short time, ordered the arms to be got out. The people on the ship were very relieved to see the land, because the water and food were very short after the five weeks that had passed since they left the Marianas the first time.

Now Guam is near the eastern limit of the zone of the south-west monsoon, which is inclined to lose its force thereabouts in the face of the prevailing north-east trade wind. Soon after Guam came in sight the wind from the north-east blew with sustained force, so that they could not make the island.

Angle, after struggling vainly against the north-east wind for some time, ordered the ship to be brought about in order to run for the Philippines again. After a time they found themselves once again frustrated by the south-west monsoon and driven back. Again they encountered the north-east wind and resumed their voyage to the Philippines. Again the south-westerlies drove them back. Yet again they got a following wind towards the Philippines for a time. Five times in all they were shuttled back and forth in this manner. On one occasion they were once more tantalized by the sight of Guam without being able to make the island.

A new horror now supervened. The *San Jeronimo* became becalmed. The terrors of heat and thirst caused the people on the ship much suffering. The soldiers wondered how Nature could be so cruel as to make the water round them so clear and inviting and yet undrinkable. Another said that just one good drink would be worth giving one's shirt for, but others thought a more fitting price would be 500 ducats.

The weather then became changeable, with occasional showers. Sheets were spread in order to catch every drop possible. But not enough was obtained to make much difference to the ration, which was a quarter of a pint a day.

At last the wind went round to the south, making it possible for the ship to run for the Philippines with the weather on the beam. The fact that ballast was short, and that most of the soldiers' chests had been left on Ujelang, meant that the ship rolled sickeningly in the cross-seas. Lope Martin was roundly cursed for hurrying the ship out of Acapulco without sufficient ballast. Martinez wrote that they could not keep their footing on the decks, or even sleep without tying themselves in.

The *San Jeronimo* was now in bad shape. She was eighteen years old, and five months at sea had not improved her. The tremendous seas did further damage, breaking the bowsprit so that it had to be lashed with rope. The ship's ribs shivered under the impact of the waves. The crew could not work the sails properly, because of the damage that had been sustained, and because the men were worn out with hunger and thirst.

On the evening of 1 October, when there was only one barrel of water left for 136 people, and very little food, the cry from the mast that all had been waiting for was raised. 'Land ahead!' It had been 55 days since they left Rota for the Philippines, a distance of 1300 miles, which Legazpi's Armada the previous year had traversed in 10 days.

The *San Jeronimo* had struck the Philippines near San Bernardino Strait, between Samar and Luzon. This was a bit of luck, since instead of being faced with a lee shore they were borne by the currents through the Strait into deep open water. All round them they saw the high fertile slopes of many islands, abounding in rivers and streams. On 4 October they found anchorage at a small island, and the ship's boat went in to the shore for water and supplies.

On this day, when relief was in sight, the people on the ship felt the pangs of thirst more than ever. It was very hot, and some of the men, while awaiting the return of the boat, fell to drinking sea-water. Had they had to pass another such day, some of them, it was felt, would have died.

Meanwhile Santiago de Garnica and Juan de Enrique had gone ashore as leaders of the landing-party. As they neared the beach, they saw a village on a point, surrounded by crude protective earthworks. The presence of pigs and fowls showed there would be both food and water there.

As the Spaniards landed they were received with open hostility by the villagers, who threw stones and spears at them from within the earthworks.

It was decided that the landing-party should shoot its way into the village. The musketeers proceeded to the task, nor

did the defenders fail in courage. Before the villagers broke
and fled, fifteen of them were killed.

When the landing-party entered the deserted village, they
drank and ate for a time like men possessed. Then they
searched the huts, looking for the gold in which the Philippines were reputed to abound. But if anything of value had
been possessed by these islanders, it had been removed by
them when they fled.

Having drunk and eaten their fill, the foragers filled their
casks from a stream, and gathered some food for the ship.
The thirst and hunger of those who had remained on the
ship was thus at last relieved.

Angle, Garnica and Enrique now decided to stay at this
island for some time. They put most of the people ashore
under Garnica's supervision. Angle remained in charge of
the ship.

During the week that the ship was there, quantities of
water, rice, goats, fowls and fruit, as well as ballast, were
loaded into the ship.

One day a mischief-making sailor had some conversation
with Garnica on shore. He advised Garnica not to trust the
soldiers, saying that some of them were planning to kill him.

Such was the tension that still permeated the minds of the
leaders that Garnica, without waiting to inquire into this
report, went out to Angle on the ship and repeated the
accusation. Angle, ever willing to lend an ear to anything
that accorded with his own suspicions and anxieties, said he
would hang six or eight of the ringleaders and disarm the
rest of the soldiers.

When Angle planned to initiate some strong-arm action,
however, he found that he no longer had any great amount
of power to his elbow. For one thing the soldiers were now
armed because of the threat of attack from the local Filipinos.
Secondly Angle's navigating talents were no longer vital to a

landfall. Indeed it had become obvious to all that Angle did
not quite know where they were in relation to Legazpi's
camp at Zebu. So his bent for reprisals came to nothing. As
for the supposed conspiracy against Garnica, there was no
evidence that it was anything more than a piece of irrespons-
ible rumour, like many of the informers' statements which
were rife on the *San Jeronimo*.

At the end of the week at this island, Angle determined to
go south to latitude $10\frac{1}{3}$ degrees, which was the latitude of
Legazpi's camp. It was hoped that Garnica, who had come
from Zebu to Mexico with the *San Pedro* the previous year,
might recognize the local topography of Zebu.

Some of the pessimists among the soldiers thought that
Angle would be by no means put out if it were found that
Legazpi had abandoned the settlement.

The next morning Garnica and Enrique with sixteen men
set off in the ship's boat ahead of the *San Jeronimo*. The idea
was that they should seek out some place where they could
forage for more food, and then rejoin the ship as it passed
south. When they came to a pleasant fertile part of the coast
of one island, they went ashore and found some food, on
which they regaled themselves. When they came out again
they looked for the ship, but it was nowhere to be seen.
Owing to the over-long time they had spent in their feasting,
Angle had in fact passed them, thinking they were farther
ahead.

Angle now had to make for the south in the inner sea of
the Philippines without the benefit of such help as Garnica
and his companions might have given, and without the ship's
boat. Garnica and Enrique and the men in the boat with
them were lost in the heart of the Philippines.

Angle and the company of the *San Jeronimo*, continuing on
to the south, looking out for the lost boat all the time, came
within ten miles of the north-west coast of an island which

was in fact Zebu, although they did not know it at the time. They were actually heading for the west or wrong side of Zebu, with an excellent chance of missing Legazpi's camp for an indefinite period, if not for ever.

Suddenly a sail was seen to port. It was a small craft of some sort. Some of the people on the *San Jeronimo* thought it must be the ship's boat with Garnica and his party. Others, perhaps thinking of loot, suggested it might be a junk.

Angle gave the order to change course so as to meet the strange vessel. As the gap closed, it became obvious that it was not a junk, but a European ship's boat. Everybody now thought it was the ship's boat with the missing men.

While the boat was still some distance from the *San Jeronimo*, instead of coming on, it stood off and then passed beyond the ship, positioning itself astern of it. It was plain that the people in the boat were unsure of the *San Jeronimo*, and that the boat was not in fact that of the *San Jeronimo* at all.

The commander of the boat now spoke to the ship, saying that he was Captain Juan de la Isla of the Armada of Captain-General Legazpi of Spain.

Great was the joy on the *San Jeronimo* at this fortunate encounter. The cheers from the soldiers and sailors almost drowned Angle's identification of the *San Jeronimo*. It was indeed some time before Isla was sufficiently satisfied to come aboard.

It was now agreed that Isla should stay on board and guide them to Legazpi at Zebu Town some 100 miles away on the other side of Zebu. Isla sent his boat ahead to tell the joyful news to the Captain-General.

As Isla and Angle brought the ship toward Legazpi's camp, Isla explained the lucky chance that had brought him to the north of Zebu. Legazpi had sent Captain Saz in one of the ship's boats to Leyte, to the north-east of Zebu, some time previously. When Captain Saz did not come back within the due time, Isla went in search of him. Instead of finding Captain Saz, Isla had met the *San Jeronimo*.

When the ship's boat sent ahead by Isla reached Zebu Town, Saz had already got there safely, having missed Isla on the way. The news of the coming of the *San Jeronimo* caused Legazpi and Saz much joy. They were doubly pleased to know that the *San Pedro* with Felipe de Salcedo and Andres de Urdaneta had reached Mexico safely, even though they had been unable to secure the despatch of Arellano and the *San Lucas* to Legazpi.

Captain Saz then went in the pinnace to meet the approaching *San Jeronimo* and escort her into the port.

When the voyagers arrived, Martinez described the celebrations that marked the end of their travail: 'It is not possible to do justice to the contentment and pleasure which were felt by everybody from the Governor to the humblest person, for they were so delighted that some wept and others laughed for joy, others raced round, and others again, forgetful of their former enmities, became friends again. Bells were rung and the band played, and the monks gave great thanks in the Church along with the Governor.'

Thus ended the spectacular voyage of the *San Jeronimo*, on 15 October, 1566, at Zebu, after five and a half months of mutiny, murder, durance, thirst, hunger, hatred and tears. What a sight she must have made as, with flags flying on ship and shore, her timbers crazed, her masts all either broken or cracked, she was hailed by a salvo of artillery from the shore as she staggered into Port Zebu on what was to be her last course. Surely the *San Jeronimo* deserves a mooring in that haven of the imagination in which famous ships still ride.

The voyage was not yet over for Garnica and Enrique and their sixteen companions in the ship's boat which had been lost among the islands to the north of Zebu. After realizing that they had missed the *San Jeronimo*, they came south from island to island, until they saw a settlement with fertile plantations, pigs and fowls.

As they neared the beach close to the village, the villagers came out, but instead of throwing spears and stones, they waved what looked like papers at the boat and shouted one or two Spanish words.

The Spaniards therefore held their fire. When Garnica disembarked, the chief of the village thrust a parchment into his hand. This proved to be a document signed by Captain-General Legazpi himself. It was a testament of friendship between Legazpi, as Governor of the islands, and the chief of the village, duly attested and complete with seal.

There were cheers and shouts of joy over this, for it showed that they were not far from Legazpi's camp. This pleased the chief and villagers no less than the Spaniards, who became good friends. They all put their arms away, and celebrated the occasion by feasting, Europeans and Filipinos together, on pigs, fowls, fruit and coconut wine.

Such were the attractions of the little settlement that Garnica and Enrique were in no hurry to leave. They and their men were in need of rest and recuperation. The chief told them that when they were ready to go he would send some of his people with them to show them the way.

In due course Garnica and his companions, accompanied by some guides from the village, came south again, being met on the way by a pinnace sent by Legazpi to look for them. They arrived at Zebu some seventeen days after the *San Jeronimo*.

Legazpi now showed his magnanimity by giving all the company of the *San Jeronimo* except one a free pardon in the name of the King for any peccadilloes they might have been guilty of. He said that all the mutineers except one had already paid the penalty either of death or exile on the unknown island in the ocean. Angle's aberration in being willing to follow Lope Martin in order to save his own life was considered to be atoned for by his achievement in bringing the *San Jeronimo* eventually in safety to Zebu. The one exception to the amnesty was Juan de Zaldivar, the scribe, whose luck finally ran out. He was executed after confessing he had aided the mutineers by telling them the secrets given to him as scribe by Pericon, and by giving some of them arms. He should have stuck to his quill.

10

Skulduggery at Zebu

DURING the sixteen months at Zebu between the departure of the *San Pedro* on 1 June, 1565, and the arrival of the *San Jeronimo* on 15 October, 1566, many curious and interesting things had been happening in the Philippines.

It will be remembered that at the time the *San Pedro* left, Tupas and the other chiefs of Zebu had ignored or evaded Legazpi's overtures. One of Legazpi's company of gentlemen, Pedro de Arana, had been assassinated on the very beach of Zebu Town, and a punitive expedition had brought back some captives, including two women and two girls of chiefly rank, to the Spanish camp. These ladies were being held in custody in a hut in the camp, where they were being treated with every courtesy.

Legazpi and his advisers now had some conversation about their next move. They decided to use the captives as an inducement to Tupas to treat with them. One of the women was the wife of Tupas's brother Simaquio, and the two girls were their daughters.

Another woman who had been captured with Simaquio's womenfolk was accordingly sent with a white cloth as a flag of peace to find Tupas and the other chiefs.

The next day a Moslem resident of Zebu named Sidamit came to the camp bringing the white cloth. He spoke both Malay and the local language and could therefore talk with Legazpi through his Malay-speaking interpreter.

Sidamit asked what amount of gold the Spaniards wanted as ransom for the women. Legazpi answered that they did not wish to take ransom for them at all. They were being kept in custody only until Tupas and the other chiefs came to make peace, and were being well treated.

To show that this was true, Legazpi arranged for Sidamit to be taken to the hut where the ladies were, where he ascertained for himself that they were well and happy.

Sidamit then asked if permission would be given for Simaquio to come and see his wife and daughters. Legazpi replied that he would be made very welcome.

Next day Simaquio and another chief came to the camp, accompanied by Sidamit as interpreter, with twenty or twenty-five followers.

Simaquio said that he had come so that Legazpi might do anything he wished with him, provided he spared his wife and daughters. Simaquio would go with them as a slave to their own country if the Spaniards wished.

Legazpi assured Simaquio that all he wanted was that Tupas and the other chiefs should come and make a treaty of friendship with him.

Simaquio himself was now conducted to his womenfolk, who told him they were being treated with great courtesy. The chief was greatly pleased, raising his eyes and hands to the skies as a sign of gratitude. Simaquio was moved by this liberality on the part of Legazpi to say that he would be a loyal vassal of the King of Spain.

Simaquio then returned to his people, and the next day returned with Tupas's son, a fine-looking youth of about twenty.

Legazpi had given Simaquio's wife and daughters blouses of Rouen lace, in which they preened themselves before Simaquio. Simaquio was allowed to stay the night with them, while Tupas's son went home, saying that his father and the other chiefs would come the following day.

The Spaniards, wishing to do everything possible to impress the chiefs when they came, dressed Simaquio as well as the ladies in fine Spanish clothes. Simaquio wore a jacket of Rouen lace, breeches of taffeta, and a handsome hat. As presents for Tupas and the other chiefs, other fine raiment was got ready.

At noon the next day, finally reassured, Tupas and seven other chiefs, with fifty to seventy followers, duly appeared at the camp, where Legazpi received them with every show of friendship.

Legazpi addressed the chiefs, saying that Zebu was under the power of the King of Spain, who desired that they be his loyal subjects. In return the King, through Legazpi as his Governor, would protect and aid them against their enemies, and they would do mutually profitable trade.

Tupas and the other chiefs put their weapons on the ground before Legazpi and kissed his hands, saying that they would be vassals of Spain. Tupas was then given a shirt of Rouen lace, a jacket and breeches of purple damask, a sombrero of blue silk, a silver belt, a large mirror, and two strings of pearls, while the other chiefs were given similar finery. Legazpi then gave a feast in celebration of the occasion. Finally Simaquio's wife and daughters were delivered over to their men, who carried them off shoulder-high amid singing and shouting.

The men and women of Zebu now came back to the town near the Spanish camp, and became very friendly with the soldiers there.

This friendship soon had undesirable results in the eyes of Legazpi's officers. The local people were bringing huge quantities of palm wine into the camp, and they and their women were drinking with the men at all hours of the day and night in the soldiers' quarters.

An order was accordingly issued forbidding the trade in liquor, but every effort to enforce it was defeated. 'This wine's better than that of Castile, and more sustaining,' was the common opinion of the soldiers and sailors, who appeared to think it was all the sweeter when poured by the hands of the ladies of Zebu.

Some of these ladies divulged that they were priestesses of a devilish cult. They explained that they had the power to make a demon enter into a hollow cane and speak to them from it, whereupon the faithful were invited by the priestesses to make offerings of pigs, fowls and other presents.

One day Tupas came to Legazpi to make a suggestion. He said that his wife and daughters were envious that Simaquio's wife and daughters should have been so well received by Legazpi, and were always urging Tupas to ask Legazpi to let them come and pay their respects too. Legazpi answered that nothing would give him greater pleasure.

Tupas and his womenfolk and their retainers then put on a very fine parade. They came in procession to the camp. First came seventy women walking two by two, all of them chanting in a high voice, most of them wearing palm sombreros on their heads, others garlands of flowers. They all wore skirts and mantles of various hues, and gold ornaments. After these women came Tupas's wife, with her ladies-in-waiting. Tupas and his men came separately.

After feasting his visitors, Legazpi gave Tupas's wife and daughters-in-law and nieces some Rouen lace, pearl beads, mirrors and Spanish combs, and the other women crystal beads and other trinkets. Then the procession re-formed and went off to the accompaniment of singing.

This naturally started a spate of requests from the wives of other chiefs of Zebu for a series of similar ceremonies, all of

F

which Legazpi granted with his wonted courtesy. In order to relieve the strain on the official supplies of presents, he contributed much cloth and other gifts from his own coffers.

Tupas now sent to the Governor one of his nieces, attended by three serving-women, with the intention that she should be a member of his household. The devout Legazpi arranged that she should be instructed in Christian doctrine, and she expressed a desire to be baptized. When the monks were satisfied that her intentions were sincere, she was duly received into the Church with the name of Isabel. This opened up the way, not only for a number of conversions and baptisms, but also for a romance.

Maestre Andrea, a Greek sailor, having found his heart smitten with the charms of the dusky Isabel, confided to Legazpi and the monks that he desired her hand in holy wedlock. This was in due course arranged, and Legazpi took advantage of the occasion to put on a fine wedding, to which the chiefs of Zebu were invited. This heart-warming event caused a noticeable acceleration in the applications of the local ladies for religious instruction.

Now while things had been going forward so encouragingly at Port Zebu itself, the villages farther afield were more recalcitrant. Mactan and Gavi were the main centres of the trouble, as they had been since the beginning. Their chiefs were strengthened by the memory of past glory, when they had successfully carried off the head of Pedro de Arana. They kept taunting the people who had accepted the Spaniards with their cowardice in letting them settle there. On one occasion some canoes from Mactan and Gavi crept into the port under highly suspicious circumstances, and when they were discovered took refuge with the people of Zebu Town itself. The chiefs of Zebu Town, Gavi and Mactan all had ties of kinship. After a time it became plain that the loyalties of Tupas and his people were in fact divided, although they were

sufficiently impressed by the power of the Spaniards not to
cause trouble openly.

Because of the considerable demands for food involved in
providing for some 200 men, it was becoming increasingly
hard to get adequate supplies in the vicinity of Port Zebu.
Therefore there now began a series of foraging expeditions
to other places. This became part of the continuing pattern of
Legazpi's occupation of Zebu, and Saz and the other captains
were frequently away on these voyages to more distant parts
in search of food.

Other expeditions were made to help Tupas and his people
against their enemies. These had the result of showing both
parties the force of Spanish arms. Great was the impression
made by Saz on the first of these punitive raids in support of
Tupas. The Spaniards assaulted a well-defended position on a
slope, and by good planning and discipline, aided by their
coats of mail and steel helmets, managed to take it in the face
of a hail of stones, spears and arrows. It was indeed hard to
separate peaceful penetration and trade from force of arms,
and force of arms from conquest.

One day a trader from Manila in Luzon, the northern and
most advanced island in the Philippines, came to Zebu. This
contact was in due course to have a powerful influence on the
Spanish destinies in the Philippines. His first meeting with
Legazpi and the Crown officials was a droll event in the
history of commerce.

The trader's name was Mahomet. Like most of the
Moslems of the Philippines, he had acquired a smattering of
Mohammedanism from the Moslems of Borneo, but was a
native Filipino. Having come to Zebu Town in a canoe
with six or seven followers, Mahomet was taken to Legazpi.
He explained that he was a trading captain who had been sent
by Raja Soliman, Chief of Manila, to the north of Zebu
Island, where he had heard of the presence of the Spaniards

at Zebu Town. He had therefore come in a canoe in order to
see whether they would allow him to bring his large trading
vessel to do business with them.

Legazpi said that Mahomet and his trading canoe would be
made very welcome, and gave Mahomet some scarlet
bonnets and other presents. In three days Mahomet was
back with his large trading *parao*, which was a wide shallow-
draught vessel depending on oars and sails. In it he had
Chinese iron and porcelain, as well as Philippine gold and
rice.

Mahomet then looked over the Spanish trade goods, comprising silks, linens, iron, tin, copper, silver, pearls and
trinkets. Mahomet's assessment was that only the silver and
pearls were of any great value to him, since the other types
of goods were brought in quantity to Luzon by the Chinese
junks.

Some lively bargaining now ensued. A stiff price in silver
was charged by Mahomet for his rice, for he knew that food
was scarce with the Spaniards. When the food had gone,
Mahomet offered gold at the rate of one part by weight for
five parts of silver, but the Spaniards declined because the
gold was impure. It was then agreed that Mahomet's gold
would be bought for pearls at the same rate of exchange.

The officials were supervising the weighing of the pearls
when Mahomet intervened. He said that he was interested
only in the small pearls and asked that these be selected for
him. This apparently strange request was in due course
explained when Mahomet divulged that it was because it was
customary for them to sell pearls by count and not by weight.

This suggestion was however embarrassing to the Spaniards,
since they had few small pearls. They therefore insisted that
Mahomet take the pearls as they came, both big and small.

As the pearls were being weighed again, Mahomet had a
fit of sneezing. He then said that the deal was off, so far as

the pearls were concerned, because it was a bad omen to sneeze, and the custom of his country was to desist from business in the face of so grave a portent.

While Mahomet was in the vicinity of Zebu Town, the Spaniards found that the local people refused to take anything but silver for their pigs, fowls and other food. It was plain that Mahomet had put them up to this, promising them good bargains for handing the silver on to him. But since Mahomet used his influence to get the villages farther off to send food, the Spaniards indulged him, and got needed supplies as a result. Mahomet, in fact, was adjudged a very useful and popular fellow.

The mischief-making of the chiefs of Mactan and Gavi came to a head at about this time. One day a fire broke out in one of the soldiers' huts. Before the resulting conflagration could be got under control, twenty buildings had been destroyed. Among them were the quarters of the monks, who lost much of their property. When inquiries were made into how this fire started, suspicion fell on the people of Mactan. It was accordingly agreed that Saz and Goite should take a party of soldiers and have things out with the recalcitrants. But when they got to Mactan the captains found it deserted, without even household goods or other property, which made the Spaniards think that the people of Zebu Town had warned their neighbours of the wrath to come.

Saz and Goite then put the torch to the houses of Mactan. The wheel had come full circle from the time when Magellan and his men had been repulsed from Mactan with the loss of the commander himself.

The captains found also that the people of Gavi, the other main trouble spot, had also decamped. It was found later that most of the fugitives from Mactan and Gavi had gone off to the east coast of Samar, although it was suspected that quite a few had found refuge with their friends and relatives in and around Port Zebu.

The refugees from Mactan and Gavi who fled to Samar were certainly not lacking in persistence. Some time later they persuaded their hosts of Samar to join them in a raid on a village about a league from the Spanish camp at Zebu, the people of this village being friendly to the Spaniards. The raiders carried off as captives more than thirty prisoners. Thereupon the people of the village fled to the interior of Zebu Island. Legazpi, feeling that the prestige of Spain was involved, sent Saz on a punitive expedition to Samar. Saz had little success in rescuing the villagers who had been captured, but showed the flag to such effect that numbers of the people of Zebu who had fled to Samar decided they could not dodge the Spaniards anyway, and therefore came back. The chiefs of Mactan and Gavi, however, remained defiant at Samar, whence they exhorted their compatriots at Zebu and the neighbouring islands not to co-operate with the invaders by supplying food.

The greatest trial that beset Legazpi and his officers in these middle months of 1566, however, was occasioned by the machinations of the foreign pilots who had come with the Armada. It will be remembered that the Frenchman Pierres Plun, the Venetians Jaymes Fortun and Juan Maria, and Jorge the Greek, together with Lope Martin, had been the ringleaders in a conspiracy in La Navidad to seize the *San Lucas* and go off in search of gold and spices on their own account. In these plots they had enlisted the support of a Venetian corporal of the military named Pablos Hernandez. Various other foreigners, and some Spaniards too, had secretly been suborned by the schemers, to the number of some forty in all. Their schemes had been thwarted for one reason and another in La Navidad and on the high seas, and following on the disappearance of the *San Lucas* the rest of the plotters had come willy-nilly to Zebu.

Since coming to Zebu, the conspirators had been waiting

for a chance to pursue their plan, the object of their piratical enterprise being the smaller of the remaining ships, the *San Juan*. Following on the disappearance of the *San Lucas* and the return of the *San Pedro* to Mexico, the big galleon, the *San Pablo*, and the *San Juan*, remained at Zebu. Not a great number of men were needed to seize and make off with the *San Juan*. Part of the plan was to scuttle the *San Pablo* and the pinnaces. The intention then was to secure a load of gold and spices and then sail either to France or to the Portuguese in the East Indies.

Pablos Hernandez, as the senior soldier among the plotters, was to be the captain, while Juan Maria, who as the master of the *San Pablo* had control of the ship's arms and stores of ammunition, was to be second-in-command.

The plans of the plotters being finally laid, a night was set for the execution of the coup. Hernandez and the soldiers in the plot being in the camp on land, Juan Maria and Jaymes Fortun on the *San Pablo* started the first steps by loading some arms and supplies into the ship's boat. Some of the sailors on the *San Pablo* who were not in the conspiracy, when they noted these actions, expressed some surprise to the pilot, Jaymes Fortun. To their inquiry Fortun answered that they were carrying out orders.

At this point the conspirators decided to postpone their attempt until the following night. The reason is not entirely clear, but from what Juan Maria did next day it seems probable that Maria lost his nerve.

Next morning Maria presented himself to Captain Saz. He reported that Hernandez and their fellow-conspirators had for some time past been plotting to seize the *San Juan*. Maria said that he had decided to reveal the plot and throw himself on Saz's mercy.

To this Saz answered that he would see that Maria was pardoned for saving them from the grave threat that had been revealed by him in the nick of time.

Meanwhile Hernandez remained in ignorance of the fact that he had been betrayed.

When Saz reported the plot to Legazpi, the leader was very angry. He gave orders that Hernandez should be seized and made to confess all his accomplices. It was agreed that Saz should wait till evening before seizing Hernandez so that there would be no overt indication that the conspiracy had been discovered.

Guards were accordingly placed on the gates, and as soon as it was dark Captain Saz took a party of soldiers to Hernandez's hut to seize him, but he was not there. Another soldier, meeting Hernandez, told him Saz and a party of soldiers were searching for him. Hernandez realized that the plot had been discovered, and hid in a thicket in the vicinity.

When Legazpi heard that Hernandez could not be found, he told Saz to elicit from Maria the names of Hernandez's friends, so that they could be questioned.

Juan Maria then betrayed others of his fellow-conspirators as he had already betrayed Hernandez. Pierres Plun, the French pilot, Jorge the Greek, and a number of others were seized on Maria's information. Sad to relate, Andrea the Greek, the newly wedded spouse of Isabel, whose nuptials Legazpi had celebrated so lavishly, was among them. Another was a Frenchman, Guillermo de la Fosa, who in order to save his own life was in his turn particularly forthcoming in information about the plot and his fellows in it.

As dawn broke, the hangings began. First Pilot Plun was strung up, then Jorge the Greek. Andrea was to be next, and was being confessed, when the monks and some of the captains decided to plead with Legazpi that the lives of the rest of the conspirators be spared. They pointed out that they needed all the men they had.

Finally Legazpi agreed to be merciful to all but Hernandez.

Isabel was spared the pangs of early widowhood, and the rest of the men were admonished and freed.

Now came a pursuit of the wretched Hernandez, whose countryman and false friend Juan Maria had betrayed him without warning.

First Hernandez took refuge in the monks' quarters, begging that he be allowed to become an initiate to save his life. But the monks said it was not fitting, since the Governor had proscribed him as ringleader. They did not however give him away. Hernandez then took refuge in the hut of one of the Filipinos in the village. The villagers, however, had been warned by the Spaniards to seize the fugitive if they saw him and deliver him alive to the camp. So Hernandez's host, having given him some food and taken possession of his knife, went off to get some of his neighbours to help seize the wanted man. Hernandez, hearing them coming, fled into the thickets.

Hernandez then managed to get back to the monks, and they agreed to intercede with Legazpi for his life, giving him temporary sanctuary. But Legazpi would not agree, standing firm on his decision that an example must be made of Hernandez as the leader of the plotters. It must be conceded that a conspiracy to sink the one remaining galleon and steal the last ship was no small crime.

Finally Hernandez gave himself up, asking that his execution be put off till noon the next day so that he could make a full confession, which he accordingly made to Saz. He was then publicly executed, and his head was impaled on a stake by the gallows as a horrid example of the results of mutiny.

The months wore by, with continual shortages of food, despite the incessant foraging to other islands in the vicinity of Zebu.

After a while the grisly deterrent of Hernandez's head on the stake was forgotten. Discontent, increased by hunger, again motivated some of the trouble-makers.

It started with Juan Nuñez de Carrion, one of Legazpi's company of gentlemen. He had already a very chequered record. He had been condemned at one stage for some crime by Saz, but had been reprieved by Legazpi. He had been implicated in the recent mutiny, but had been pardoned under Legazpi's general amnesty. It was generally agreed in the camp that he was a disagreeable fellow, arrogant and quarrelsome.

One of the people with whom Carrion had had some words was another of Legazpi's company of gentlemen named Francisco Arias Maldonado. Yet they had made up their quarrel and appeared to be friends again. Such however were the contortions of Carrion's mind that, being already very discontented with the privations in the camp, he conspired to desert to the Portuguese in the Moluccas and at the same time give himself the pleasure of murdering Maldonado before he went.

Carrion approached a malefactor named Chavez, whom Legazpi had had flogged a few days before for having robbed and ill-treated some of the local Filipinos. Chavez agreed to throw in his lot with Carrion. So did one Miguel Gomez, who had been confined for theft. Carrion also approached several others. One of these was Guillermo de la Fosa, a Frenchman who had been involved in the recent mutiny. To Fosa Carrion offered the leadership, and Fosa said he would accept.

Carrion explained his plans to his accomplices. Mahomet, the trader from Luzon, was due to leave Port Zebu in his big trading canoe the following day. Carrion knew that Mahomet's first stopping-place would be about ten miles to the north. He therefore proposed to hide some arms along the coast a bit. Then when the Luzon traders left, the conspirators would follow them along the coast, picking up the arms without anybody being any the wiser, and would then seize the big canoe. On it there would be all the supplies they could want, and they could then go in it to the Portuguese station in the Moluccas to the south-east of the Philippines.

Carrion accordingly got some arms and ammunition on the pretext that he was organizing a hunting trip, and secreted them at a safe distance along the coast.

The following day the Luzon traders left Port Zebu on their way north. Everything was ready for Carrion's plan to be put into effect when dark fell. They would make their way along the coast, picking up the muskets on the way, and would fall on Mahomet and his trading canoe at their stopping-place to the north. Carrion, as a parting piece of vindictive-ness, planned to murder Maldonado just before he left.

Meanwhile Guillermo de la Fosa, the Frenchman to whom Carrion, for what his word was worth, had offered the leadership, was telling everything to Legazpi.

Carrion and Gomez were seized forthwith, and confessed the whole plot. Chavez managed to escape, and, fleeing after the very Luzon traders he had conspired to despoil, begged them to take him with them to Luzon. But while they did not know of his villainies, they refused to assist him as a deserter because of their good relations with Legazpi. Chavez then tried to hide, but was found and seized, and confessed his complicity with Carrion.

Soon Carrion's and Chavez's heads were on stakes beside the gallows.

Some time after these treasons had been quelled, a more heart-warming diversion took place. Captain Martin de Goite had been sent to the eastern islands of the Philippines to look for supplies of rice. When he was in the vicinity of the narrow strait which divides Leyte from Samar, he heard from the local people that a Spaniard named Juanes had been living in a village nearby for more than twenty years. When

Goite went to the village the people had fled. Goite however brought back with him three captives taken near this village.

Legazpi treated the three prisoners with his customary kindness, and soon had their confidence. They explained that Juanes belonged to a chief named Sibuco, who regarded him as his son. Juanes had come a long time before in a small European boat which had been wrecked on their coast.

The Spaniards at Zebu knew from this that Juanes must be a survivor from a pinnace which had been lost during Villalobos's expedition to the Philippines over a score of years before.

Part of Legazpi's instructions were to look for any survivors of previous Spanish expeditions to the Isles of the West. Sentiment was also very much on the side of rescuing Juanes as a compatriot.

Legazpi accordingly sent Captain Saz in some of the ships' boats and pinnaces to rescue Juanes. Saz's former captives, now free men returning to their home, accompanied Saz as willing allies in securing the release of Juanes. The treasurer, Guido de la Bezares, went along with Saz also with a plentiful supply of gold and trinkets as a ransom to be paid for Juanes in accordance with Philippine custom.

Now it happened that one Pedro de Herrera had been sent on an independent visit to Samar to get some resin as a substitute for pitch, of which there was a great need for caulking the seams in the wooden ships. Soon after Saz had gone off on his search for Juanes, Herrera returned to Zebu with an intriguing and indeed alarming story of three more Spanish captives.

When he was on the south coast of Samar, reported Herrera, he met a family living on a large canoe. They told him through the interpreters that they were itinerant fisherfolk who had no home on land. There were, they said, a number of canoes in the Philippines with families living like themselves. They caught fish and went the rounds of the coastal villages selling it for food and other goods, living on the canoe with no home or settled place of abode. The people called them Lutaos. The Lutao family told Herrera that they had seen three Spaniards like himself in the north of Samar. They had been captured from a ship fourteen or fifteen months before.

This news caused Legazpi much perturbation, since it looked very much as if these further Spanish exiles were survivors from the *San Pedro*, which had set out for Mexico the previous year under the captaincy of Legazpi's grandson Felipe, and his kinsman Urdaneta.

Legazpi decided to send Captain Juan de la Isla in one of the ship's boats in search of Saz, in order to tell him to try to rescue these other three Spaniards as well as Juanes. Isla, however, missed Saz, but met the *San Jeronimo* coming from Mexico, as told in the previous chapter. When Isla got back to Zebu with the *San Jeronimo*, Saz had already returned there from Leyte.

In the meantime Saz had set about the rescue of Juanes with his usual determination. He got his Filipino allies to make contact with Sibuco, the owner-father of Juanes, at his village, and tell him the Spaniards were determined to have Juanes, and were prepared to pay a good ransom for him. Such was the attachment of Sibuco to his adopted son that he was keeping him tied up and in hiding. But when the strength of the visitors' forces, combined with the promise of gold and other fine gifts, finally won him over, he sent Juanes to Saz with an escort in a canoe.

As the canoe approached, the Spaniards, who were waiting on a beach, were much affected to hear Juanes call out to them '*Yo creo en Dios* (I believe in God)'. Then Juanes leapt out on the shore before Saz, put the lance he was carrying on the ground, raised his hands and eyes to Heaven, and said '*O bendito y alabado sea mi Dios todo poderoso* (Blessed and exalted be my God the all-powerful)'. Then he and Saz embraced each other.

These demonstrations of Christian sentiment, made in the mother-tongue of their common homeland, as Saz thought, greatly moved him. He asked Juanes a number of questions in Spanish, but found that all he could say in that language were a few religious phrases learned in his youth. A greater surprise awaited Saz, for Juanes was not a Spaniard at all, but a Mexican Indian who had come with Villalobos's expedition as a youthful serving-lad to a Spaniard named Juan Crespo. He had been baptized as a Christian in Mexico, and remembered his Creed in Spanish better than his native Mexican tongue, which he had almost completely forgotten.

Juanes then conveyed his story to the Spaniards, speaking in the Philippine tongue to the interpreters, who passed on his meaning. He had come there in the boat that was wrecked with sixteen Spanish soldiers and sailors. All the others had since died, either of illness or in the local wars. The last to die, one Juan Flores, had gone with thirty men of Samar on an expedition of war about five years previously, but they were all ambushed and killed.

Of his own lot, Juanes said that he had been well treated, and had been given the daughter of a chief for his wife, by whom he had had two daughters. He had named them Catalinica and Juanita so that they might have Christian names, although he could not have them baptized. Juanes had been tattooed according to Philippine custom, and bore the marks on his flesh as a permanent souvenir.

Saz then returned to Zebu, where Juanes, as a devout Christian after so many years of exile, was received with much joy and kindness.

There was still the matter of the three Spaniards on the north coast of Samar, of whom Pedro de Herrera had heard from the Lutao. When Juanes was questioned about the reports of a wrecked ship at the time mentioned by Herrera, namely some fourteen or fifteen months previously, he could throw no light on the matter at first. But when the alleged three Spanish survivors were mentioned, he said that three Spaniards who had come in the same boat in which he himself had arrived had gone to the north of Samar, but had since died. So the mystery was cleared up. It was realized that Herrera, owing to a misunderstanding in the translation and re-translation of what the Lutao family had told him, had thought the time of the arrival of the three Spanish captives had been so many months previously when in fact it had been years.

The final relief of Legazpi's anxieties about the *San Pedro* came a day or two later, when the news of the safe arrival of the *San Pedro* in Mexico was brought by the company of the *San Jeronimo*.

I I

Alarums & Excursions

THE arrival of the *San Jeronimo* increased the manpower at
Zebu considerably. The Spaniards, over and above their
constant expeditions for food, were therefore able to go
afield searching for gold and spices. As a result they found
themselves involved in plenty of excitement.

Captain Saz went off at the beginning of November 1566
in the *San Juan* to Cavit, the south-west peninsula of Mindanao, to the south of Zebu. With him were a hundred
soldiers and sailors. Saz's instructions were to try to buy a
load of cinnamon, a spice highly prized by Europeans, made
from the dried bark of the shoots of the cinnamon tree.
Andres de Cauchela, the accountant, went along with Saz
to supervise the trading.

As the *San Juan* approached Cavit, a sail to starboard was
seen. It was a small European galiot, a vessel using both oars
and sails. When the *San Juan* drew near, the strange ship took
evasive action, moving off at a good turn of speed. When the
Spaniards saw they could not overtake it, they shortened
sail. Thereupon the other vessel did the same.

Saz then sent the sergeant in the ship's boat as an emissary.
When the sergeant was in hailing distance of the galiot, he
asked them to identify themselves. They said they were
Portuguese from India and asked who he was.

The sergeant decided to try a line of oblique diplomacy and
answered that they were Spaniards who had lost their way.

The Portuguese replied that they were at Mindanao. The sergeant then returned to the *San Juan*.

Shortly afterwards a small boat with two soldiers came from the Portuguese craft to the *San Juan*. They presented a letter, which was read by Saz with mounting feeling. It read as follows: 'I, Antonio de Sequeira, Captain of this galiot, am come to these parts by order of the Viceroy of India with Chief Captain Gonzalo de Pereira in search of one Miguel Lopez de Legazpi, who is said to have come from the east across the Pacific Ocean seeking the Moluccas. My Chief Captain, not wanting to come into these narrow waters with his big ships, has sent me to search this coast. Since you must be of Miguel Lopez de Legazpi's company, I am obliged to take steps to bring you to my Chief Captain, who will treat you well, but if you refuse I shall take hostile action.'

The gallant Saz was not the man to take such an ultimatum meekly. He indited a suitable reply and sent the Portuguese soldiers back to Captain Sequeira with it.

'Señor Captain,' wrote Saz, 'I marvel greatly at the little faith and credit you show in the Spanish nation. It is true that Governor Miguel Lopez de Legazpi came to these parts with four ships from New Spain and made a settlement at Zebu by order of His Majesty King Philip our Lord. As for your saying that we must go with your galiot, my masters would not wish it, and I, being past 25 years of age, am not afraid of your words, or deeds either. Nor do I think that His Majesty King Philip and the Very Serene King of Portugal would wish their brotherly relations to be disturbed.'

When the Portuguese captain read this, he caused a drum to be beaten and displayed flags and other signals of war. Saz then took up the challenge and bore down on the galiot. The Portuguese craft took advantage of its greater speed to draw off out of range of the *San Juan*'s guns.

Saz now decided to go back to Zebu with all haste to report the news of the Portuguese fleet to Legazpi.

For two days the *San Juan* fought contrary winds, and during this time the Portuguese galiot dogged them, keeping them in sight at a distance. Just who was dodging whom was no doubt a matter of differing opinion on the two vessels.

The following day a high gale from the south-west came up, blowing the *San Juan* at a great rate towards Zebu. They soon saw no more of the galiot. Without standing to, the Spaniards ran before the storm at great peril, in order to get back to Zebu without delay. The high seas carried away the bowsprit and the spritsail, and the gale broke the topmast.

The next evening, when the wind was still high, four galleons were seen ahead, riding out the storm, about 100 miles south of Zebu Town. They were plainly Chief Captain Pereira's Portuguese Armada from India. What had in fact happened was that Pereira had been sent by the Portuguese in India to help the Portuguese in the Moluccas to quell a rebellion in Ambon, a centre of the spice trade to the south of the Moluccas. When Pereira called at Borneo on his way to the Moluccas he heard of Legazpi's presence in the Philippines. The news of Legazpi's arrival had been brought to Borneo by the crew of the Borneo vessel which had been temporarily captured and then released by the Spaniards when they were at Bohol.

As the *San Juan* sped past the last of the galleons, it was within hailing distance, and the Spaniards called out asking what nation they belonged to. The reply came that they were Spanish. The Spaniards were not deceived at this attempt at diplomatic deception, particularly since the words were delivered with a Portuguese accent.

Still running before the wind in order to give Legazpi as much warning as possible, the *San Juan* next day, at about 30 miles from Zebu Town, saw another sinister sight. Two galiots were coasting the south-east part of Zebu Island towards Zebu Town. As the *San Juan* passed the two vessels, one of them hailed the Spaniards, who preserved a judicious silence.

That evening the *San Juan* made Zebu Town, and Saz reported to Legazpi. Immediately guards were posted and the ships were put on the alert.

The next day the two strange galiots showed up under sail at the entrance to the port, but when they saw the Spanish ships they drew out again. When a pinnace went to see what they were doing there was no sign of them.

Legazpi and his officers now decided that they must prepare against an attack by Pereira's Armada. The artillery was mounted in front of the camp so that it would command the port, and protective works, made up of barrels filled with sand and earth, were placed round the guns. The *San Pablo*, the *San Jeronimo* and the *San Juan* cleared their own decks and readied their guns. Captain Saz planned places of ambush on the sides and rear of the camp, so that if attacks were made overland a spirited resistance would await the attackers.

The soldiers and sailors entered into this with much spirit, and Legazpi gave them a pep talk, telling them the reputation of Spain was in their hands. They all agreed they would repel the attackers or die.

Meanwhile Tupas and the other chiefs of Zebu had seen these preparations with mounting apprehension. Tupas came to the Governor about it. Legazpi reassured him, saying that he would defend them. Numbers of the Filipinos joined the Spaniards in the camp, after sending off their wives and children to other villages.

This state of preparedness was maintained for three days, and then the two galiots were seen crossing the entrance to the port. They had been hiding among the shoals and islets of the nearby Mactan, and were making back to the south the way they had come.

Legazpi immediately sent Captain Goite in a pinnace to parley with them, telling him to treat them with every courtesy.

When Goite came up with the galiots, he asked them who they were, and whether they needed help. They answered that they were Portuguese, and had come with an Armada of four galleons and four galiots from India, but had been separated from the main force by the recent storm.

Goite, avoiding further query concerning the calculated character of the movements of the Portuguese galiots in their obvious search for Legazpi, then asked the visitors, in the name of Captain-General Legazpi of Spain, to enter Port Zebu, where they would be given any help and supplies they might need.

The Portuguese commander, who gave his name as Captain Melo, replied that they were in need of nothing, and would rejoin their Armada as soon as possible. Melo then said he would fire a salute and proceed on his way.

While this parley was proceeding, Goite noted that there were 35 to 40 Portuguese soldiers on each galiot, and that the crew were Indians of the Malabar coast.

Goite then returned to Legazpi while the galiots prepared to get under way. Legazpi wrote a formal letter to Melo, and sent Goite back with it. In this letter Legazpi said that he was sorry that the galiots had not come into port, where he would have welcomed them, since the orders of the King of Spain were that he should aid the Portuguese wherever he might meet them. Legazpi also sent a present of a jar of preserves, a jar of white biscuits, a jar of oil, four bottles of wine and two of vinegar. These were received by Melo with every outward appearance of goodwill. He sent a message by Goite saying that he was sorry he could not answer formally because he did not have any paper or ink. Then the two galiots sailed south to report to Pereira.

Legazpi and his captains now debated the Portuguese intentions. They felt they had good reason to fear an attack from the Armada.

The next day a comet was seen over Zebu. The soldiers were quite certain it meant war, with many deaths.

When a pinnace was sent under Sergeant Morones to the south to reconnoitre for the Portuguese fleet, however, he went as far as Mindanao without seeing any sign of it. The Spaniards concluded therefore that Pereira had gone to the Portuguese station in the Moluccas. They had little doubt, however, that sooner or later the Portuguese would be back again.

Whereas the Portuguese, by agreement with Spain, had undisputed dominion over the western areas of the East Indies, the rights of the Portuguese in respect of the Philippines were, at least in Spanish eyes, much less clear. Part of this uncertainty stemmed from the fact that there was some difference of opinion as to where the meridians of longitude in that area really lay.

As the days and weeks passed at Zebu, some intriguing happenings took place.

The old Moslem resident of Zebu Town who had served as an interpreter between Tupas and Legazpi, and who had much influence with the local Filipinos, was converted to Christianity along with his wife and family. Legazpi gave a great feast to celebrate this notable conversion, and Saz acted as sponsor.

Some of the local chiefs were influenced by this example to become Christians, but Tupas was more resistant. He said that when a Spanish fleet came bringing Spanish women, it would be time enough for him to be baptized. When inquiry was made about the reason for Tupas's attitude, it

was revealed that he did not believe unless and until Spanish
women came that the Spaniards really intended to remain,
and thought that if they baptized him they would have power
over him to remove him as a slave to Spain.

In these days the *San Jeronimo* met her end. She had been
making so much water that the pumps had to be kept working
all the time. The divers found that the keel and underparts
were so rotten that they could pick off worm-eaten pieces
with their hands. A conference of the captains and artisans
debated the fate of the ship. It was agreed that all she was
worth was to be stripped to the first deck and put on shore
to be made into a small sail-boat or a galiot. But when the
San Jeronimo was stripped of her superstructure and ballast and
put ashore, the condition of her hull was even worse than
had been thought. All her underparts were quite riddled with
decay. She was therefore broken up.

This raises the interesting speculation as to what would
have happened to Lope Martin and his fellows if they had
succeeded in going off in the *San Jeronimo* on their proposed
piratical enterprise followed by a trip to Europe.

A sad fate now overtook Juanes, the Mexican Indian who
had been rescued under dramatic circumstances by Captain
Saz. One day without warning Juanes and a Spanish sailor
named Melchior Diaz, without any obvious sickness or fever,
were seized with stomach pains, vomiting and purging, and
died in four days. The medic was quite at a loss to account
for their sudden deaths.

Five or six days later three young sailors suddenly developed the same symptoms. When the doctor questioned them,
they told him they had been given some wine to drink by
one of the women of Zebu Town, and had immediately felt
queer.

On this information the medic diagnosed poison, and
applied the same explanation retrospectively to the deaths of

Juanes and Melchior Diaz. He gave the three youths an emetic and purge, after which, though very ill for a time, they recovered.

This news upset the Governor quite a lot, particularly since there was already a standing order against the taking of wine from the local people. Furthermore the incident was considered to bring the local chiefs under suspicion.

Legazpi accordingly put out an edict that no local wine should be brought into the camp under pain of death, and guards were put on the camp gates to see that no wine was introduced.

This interdict was received with much grumbling by the company, particularly the sailors. A common sentiment among them was that they would just as soon die as give up the wine, and certainly would not be able to work or sustain themselves without it.

Legazpi then called Tupas and his fellow chiefs to hear of his sorrow and indignation. He said it pained him greatly that any of their people should reward his consideration for them so ill. Tupas and the chiefs protested that they knew nothing about the matter, but would try to find the culprits.

The next day Tupas returned with the chiefs, bringing with them two of the local women. They said these women had given wine and fish to the sailor that died, and to the youths that were sick. The women, they said, had done this out of jealousy, and when their women were jealous they frequently poisoned the people concerned, including sometimes their own husbands.

The two women were then put to the torture, whereupon they implicated two other women. These also were yielded up by the chiefs, and the four prisoners passed the blame from one to another. One of them finally confessed to having given some wine with poison in it to Melchior Diaz, while some witnesses came forward to say that the same women had given wine also to Juanes the Mexican Indian.

The stern sentence of the Court was that the woman who had confessed should be hanged and quartered, and that the other three be beaten, have their heads shaved, and be exiled permanently from Zebu. The chief culprit died as a Christian, for, having sought baptism and been granted her wish, she went to the gallows calling on God and Saint Mary with devotion.

Another application of white man's justice took place at the expense of Dagami, the chief of Gavi who had led the party who killed Pedro de Arana on the beach at Zebu and took away his head as a trophy. Dagami came once too often to Zebu, and was delivered to the Spaniards by Tupas himself, who said he was an arrogant mischief-maker. After confessing to the killing of Arana, Dagami was hanged and quartered at the spot on the beach where Arana had been killed. By a grim species of poetic justice, his head was put on a pale at this same spot.

First-hand evidence of the treasure that awaited the Spaniards in the mountains and streams of the Philippines was found by Saz and Goite early in 1567. They were at Leyte buying provisions for the camp, when one of the Leyte chiefs besought their support against his enemies on the island of Masbate, to the north of Leyte and Zebu. When the soldiers went to Masbate, the people had fled to the mountains in the interior, but the Spanish captains made some more exciting discoveries.

As Saz and Goite were exploring Masbate, they came on a village which had been deserted by its occupants on their approach. Goite, who had gone ahead with a scouting party, had some news for Saz when he arrived. Near the village were gold mines and iron tools, with provision for washing and assaying. The workings were very well constructed, with numbers of thatched huts nearby to show that the mining was systematic.

The captains marked these mines for closer attention later. The presence of gold in quantity in the Philippines meant that the conquerors could count on a rich harvest in course of time, provided they could hold on in the face of the expected Portuguese attempts to dislodge them.

It was now decided to resume the investigation of the cinnamon at Cavit in the south-west of Mindanao, which had been interrupted when Captain Sequeira's Portuguese galiot had encountered the *San Juan* the previous year. Cavit was the Cape of Cinnamon which had excited the imagination of the Europeans since the time of Magellan. It was the Zamboanga area of Mindanao.

Saz again went in the *San Juan*, together with a pinnace. His instructions were, if he met any Portuguese, to give them all possible help and courtesy for prudence's sake.

Saz accordingly sailed in the *San Juan* on 19 February, 1567, with eighty men. The other senior officers were Juan de Morones and Gaspar Ramirez. They went south to Mindanao and passed down its west coast to Cavit, where Saz had met the Portuguese galiot on his previous voyage. They sailed into the port, and saw a settlement with numbers of canoes on the beach.

The pinnace went in to the land with thirty soldiers. As it neared the beach, some thirty canoes came out to meet it. A chief in one of the canoes came close to the pinnace, and indicated that he would give them friendly co-operation.

By this time the canoes accompanying the chief were near the pinnace. Suddenly the whole scene changed. At a signal from the chief the men in the canoes seized their lances and started hurling them at the pinnace. In a very short time nearly every man in it was wounded, and the pinnace was in grave danger of being boarded and captured forthwith.

G

In this crisis the crew of the pinnace worked furiously to get it under sail. Slowly but surely it gathered way, and the defenders managed to hold off the attacking canoes long enough to escape. When they got back to the *San Juan*, it was found that some of the men had as many as seven or eight lance wounds. One soldier died from his injuries.

Now Saz's task was to get cinnamon, and he could not do this without the co-operation of the local people. He therefore decided to lead a landing-party himself and see if he could establish friendly relations with the people.

Saz accordingly made a landing and after much effort managed to make the inhabitants of one of the villages understand that cinnamon was what he wanted, and that when he had bought a load with trade goods acceptable to them, he and the ship would be gone. The villagers then became quite co-operative. They brought much cinnamon to the ship, but would take only the trade goods they valued. The goods for which the Cavit people showed a distinct preference were European clothes. It had indeed been noticed that when the ship arrived they had numbers of European breeches, shirts and caps, many of them obviously of Portuguese origin.

One of the things about which Saz and his associates were naturally curious was whether the people of Cavit had seen anything of the Portuguese Armada under Chief Captain Pereira. When they made inquiries from a chief of Cavit they received some interesting information. The Portuguese had indeed passed near there. The people of Basilan, an island to the south of Cavit, had in fact surprised two small boatloads of Portuguese, who had come into a river in Basilan to wash their clothes in the fresh water. Forty Portuguese had been killed, and five Malabar Indians who were with them had been sold as slaves to the people of another island called Jolo.

Saz and his officers had a strong feeling from this information that the Portuguese clothes which had been worn by the people of Cavit had come from their friends on Basilan, being part of the spoils taken from the Portuguese who had been attacked there.

Saz was much taken with the idea of going to Jolo and ransoming the five Indians there, since this would be a token of friendship toward the Portuguese befitting Saz's instructions to help them as much as possible. Saz's plan was to send the Indians to the Portuguese in the Moluccas after they had been rescued.

Next day, however, when they tried to find out from the people of Cavit where Jolo was, they received the most varying information, and decided to give up the project. Actually Jolo is one of the islands to the south of Mindanao and Basilan, in the Sulu Archipelago.

The corsairs of Basilan and other islands in the Sulu Archipelago were able to harry and defy both the European and East Indian vessels which passed there on their way between Borneo and the Moluccas, because their islands and rivers were thickly covered with mangroves and undergrowth.

The official supplies of the cloth which the people of Cavit wanted in exchange for their cinnamon became exhausted when only 65 quintals of the spice had been obtained.

At this juncture Martin Hernandez, the bo'sun of the *San Juan*, decided to do some private trading for cinnamon on his own account. He accordingly sold some of his personal clothes in exchange for the spice. His fellow-sailors followed suit, and for a time did a brisk trade, selling their clothes for twenty quintals of cinnamon in all. Some of the soldiers also indulged in the trade.

When this came to Saz's ears, he was much put out. He told the ship's company that the expedition's instructions forbade such trade in competition with the official needs, and that anyone caught doing this would be put in irons and punished by the Governor when they got back to Zebu.

Great was the grumbling among the sailors and soldiers who had been doing the illicit trading. Hernandez was particularly resentful. He was a Portuguese, and had been involved in the mutiny led by his namesake Pablos Hernandez the Venetian not long before. Seeking out another disgruntled foreign sailor named Antonio Corzo, Bo'sun Hernandez proposed to him that they should engineer a plot to kill Saz, go off with the *San Juan*, and join his countrymen the Portuguese.

The persistence with which mutiny and the attempted stealing of the Spanish ships took place may incline one to think that some of the trouble arose from foreigners who were planted in the Spanish ranks as spies and saboteurs for other powers. At any rate Hernandez had little trouble in getting further support. Among his fellow-conspirators was one Sosa, whose parents were Portuguese, a fact which he had concealed at the time when he enlisted in Legazpi's Armada. It was found later that Sosa had intended to go over to the Portuguese the previous year when it was thought that Pereira's Armada was coming to Zebu. Another of the ringleaders was one Juan Rodriguez, a corporal.

Now the trouble with mutiny on a ship is that everyone is cheek by jowl, and there is a constant risk of a leakage. It thus came secretly to Saz's notice that these plots were being hatched. Saz was much upset at this development, since he was a considerate and popular leader.

There ensued on board the *San Juan* a time of great travail for Saz, Morones, Ramirez and the minority whose loyalty was above question. They kept together as far as possible and watched the rest of the ship's company for overt signs of trouble. To make things worse, a malady broke out on the ship, marked by high fever and dysentery. Saz himself was laid low with it. He and his officers now decided to return to Zebu, and the *San Juan* set sail accordingly.

Soon afterwards information came to the ears of the officers indicating that Hernandez and his supporters planned to seize the ship very soon.

Saz was by this time in bad shape from his illness. Already some of the sick men were dying. With his instinct for quick action in a crisis, Saz told Morones and Ramirez to get the loyal men, disarm all the rest of the people on board immediately, and hang Hernandez out of hand.

Morones and Ramirez thus got the advantage of surprise, for Hernandez and his minions did not know their plot had been discovered. Morones, Ramirez and the loyal men disarmed the rest of the ship's company. Then Hernandez was incontinently hanged.

Saz now perceived he was sinking fast. As a last act he handed over the command to Morones.

So died the keen soldier Mateo del Saz. He had been Legazpi's right-hand man in establishing the Spanish foothold in the Philippines in the first and crucial year.

Morones and Ramirez then decided that in view of the disaffection and disease on board, Ramirez should go ahead to Zebu in the fast-sailing pinnace to get help, while the *San Juan* followed.

To make things more secure against further treachery, half a dozen sailors and soldiers who were particularly suspect were put in irons, and were divided between the ship and the pinnace, Rodriguez and Sosa being sent ahead in the pinnace with Ramirez.

When Ramirez reached Zebu, a great gloom was cast over the Spanish camp by the news of Saz's death. This was particularly painful to Legazpi, since not only had Saz been a tower of strength to him, but also the fatherly Legazpi regarded his young officers as sons.

A party was sent in the pinnace to help Morones, and in due course the *San Juan* and the pinnace sailed into port. It remained only to punish the ringleaders. Corzo, Sosa and Rodriguez were hanged.

The diagnosis of the doctors concerning the epidemic that had befallen the *San Juan* was that the people who fell sick must have eaten too much cinnamon. This makes one wonder if their diagnoses of poisoning were invariably correct.

Martin de Goite now became second-in-command in place of Saz. He was no less able and respected, although inclined to be over-impulsive.

Legazpi and Goite were now beset by many anxieties. They wondered what the Real Audiencia was doing in Mexico, that no help came to them.

June came and went, and still it brought no sign of re-inforcements and much needed supplies from New Spain. Legazpi's patience wore thin, and he decided to send the *San Juan* to Mexico under the command of Juan de la Isla.

On 10 July, 1567, when the *San Juan* was almost ready to sail, the cry was raised that two strange vessels were coming into the port.

These two craft, as they came across the water, did indeed present a strange appearance. They were two *caracoras*, which were East Indian vessels rowed by two banks of oars, and with a sail.

Each vessel proved to be manned by a Portuguese captain and six Portuguese soldiers, with sixty native Moluccans. The captains proved to be envoys from Chief Captain Pereira and the Portuguese commander in the Moluccas.

Legazpi received cordially the senior Portuguese captain, named Rombo da Costa, and after due greetings had been exchanged, the envoy presented a letter from Chief Captain Pereira. Pereira asked that the Spaniards should vacate Zebu and come to the Moluccas, where they would be well received. The letter asserted that the Philippines were within the territories of the King of Portugal.

More ominous than the letter itself was what the Spaniards heard informally from some of the visitors. These said that the Chief Captain intended to come to Zebu with four or five galleons containing four hundred Portuguese, and with thirty Moluccan *caracoras*.

These perturbing happenings received full notice in the letters with which the *San Juan* sailed from Zebu for Mexico in late July. The official report to the Real Audiencia, after recounting the Portuguese reactions, ended thus: 'The defences we have here are very weak, because the fort is not finished, and because of the low morale of our company, and the few muskets and little ammunition we have, and almost no fuse. If they (the Portuguese) come, it will be necessary not to break with them if possible, and if they are of another mind, may God contrive what serves him most. All this risk and peril has resulted from the delay whereby help has not come from New Spain: whoever has been the cause of such delay and anxieties, may God pardon him.'

Legazpi gave an evasive reply to Pereira's note, and Costa and his *caracoras* departed.

12

To the Victors the Spoils

THE help from New Spain which Miguel Lopez de Legazpi so craved was not long denied him, for his grandson Felipe de Salcedo was already well on the way to Zebu when the *San Juan* left Zebu for Mexico. Felipe had left Mexico with two ships in April, 1567, with three hundred men and supplies. One of the ships was our old friend the *San Lucas*. In August the ships arrived at Zebu.

Great was Legazpi's joy at finding that Juan de Salcedo, Felipe's younger brother, a young soldier, had come with Felipe.

As the months passed without any sign of Chief Captain Pereira and his Portuguese fleet, the Spaniards at Zebu began to think that the Portuguese at the Moluccas must have thought better of provoking the King of Spain by harassing his officers and men in the Philippines. What Legazpi did not know was that Pereira actually sailed with his Armada from the Moluccas for Zebu in October of 1567, but was unable to get to Zebu against the seasonal north-east winds. Pereira therefore decided to defer his expedition to Zebu until the autumn of 1568, and therefore returned to the Moluccas.

Early in 1568, Legazpi called a conference of his officers. He said he thought it would be wise to send the *San Pablo* to Spain via Mexico with a load of cinnamon and samples of other goods as a present to the King. The King and his advisers would then be able to judge the value of the islands and send help accordingly, or else give other instructions.

There was general assent to this, and the pinnaces were accordingly put to work in going round the islands gathering a load for the *San Pablo*. The Zamboanga area of Mindanao was revisited for cinnamon, of which 400 quintals were put into the *San Pablo*, together with specimens of Philippine gold and other products.

On 1 July, 1568, the *San Pablo* set off for Mexico under the command of Felipe de Salcedo, with some 130 men.

About 400 Europeans in all remained at Legazpi's command in Zebu. Legazpi had only one ship, the tiny *San Lucas*. The galleon in which Salcedo had come from Mexico with the *San Lucas* had gone ashore at Zebu and had been burnt for its nails.

Chief Captain Pereira at the Moluccas was now ready to proceed again for Zebu. This time he left a little earlier in the autumn, thereby getting the advantage of the seasonal south-westerlies. His fleet consisted of four galleons, several galiots, and a few *caracoras* and other small craft. Pereira's flagship was the *San Francisco*, a large galleon with a powerful armament.

On 18 September Captain Rombo da Costa, Pereira's envoy of the previous year, sailed once again into Port Zebu, in one of the small Portuguese vessels. He said he had been separated from Pereira and was seeking shelter. He reported that Pereira was coming to Legazpi's help. Legazpi received him cordially, whereupon he departed, saying he was going to look for Pereira.

Legazpi consulted with Captain Martin de Goite and Captain Juan de Salcedo, who were now his chief officers. It was decided that they had no time to lose in preparing for trouble.

Everything was now hustle and bustle in applying the plan of defence that had been worked out the previous year. There could be no hope of opposing Pereira on the sea. It was in fact fortunate that the *San Pablo* and the *San Juan* were absent. On land, however, the Spaniards readied their artillery in strategic position to command the port, and in order to give added protection to the guns, wicker containers of native type were filled with stones as emplacements and breastworks. The late Captain Saz's scheme for military guards and ambushes on the flanks and rear of the settlement was again put into effect, and numbers of friendly Filipino chiefs came to the camp with their followers.

On 28 September Captain da Costa appeared once more in Port Zebu. He said that he had found the Portuguese fleet, which was now not far away, and presented a letter to Legazpi from Pereira. In this Pereira said that he understood that the Spaniards were in need of help, and that he was coming to give it to them. To this Legazpi replied in equally complaisant terms, saying he would be pleased to welcome Pereira and his company. Captain da Costa then returned to the Portuguese fleet.

A few days later the fleet came into Port Zebu, presenting an impressive and formidable spectacle as the galleons, headed by the *San Francisco*, sailed in, the galiots and *caracoras* skimming the water with their banks of oars.

Chief Captain Pereira now visited Captain-General Legazpi at the camp with due ceremony on both sides. Shortly thereafter Legazpi went to the *San Francisco* to return the call.

All was outwardly peace and amity between the Spaniards and the Portuguese, while they measured one another's strength and intentions.

The line of diplomacy adopted by Legazpi was that he had been forced to take shelter at Zebu, and was waiting for instructions from his home authorities before moving out.

On 14 October, Pereira sent Legazpi a stiff note. In it Pereira repeated his claim that the Philippines were Portuguese territory, and bade the Spaniards either come away with him in his ships, in which case every courtesy and assistance would be given them, or else take the consequences.

The next day Legazpi replied saying that the King of Spain had told him to sail to the Isles of the West outside the Moluccas and other Portuguese domains, and that this implied that in the King's view the area occupied by Legazpi was Spanish territory. If, however, Pereira would give him two ships, he would be prepared to move out. Otherwise he must wait for ships and instructions.

Pereira replied in a further note, saying that he was amazed that Legazpi should ask him for two ships 'as a sword for cutting off my own head.'

Legazpi and his captains now decided to mount some artillery on the bank of the river so as to cover the watering-place there. This had up till that time been used both by the Portuguese and Spaniards.

When Pereira saw this, he was mightily annoyed, and sent a demand to Legazpi to desist from these preparations. This Legazpi did, for the sake of prudence.

The next morning, 20 October, Legazpi got a further note from Pereira, demanding that the works which had already been constructed at the watering-place should be destroyed by nightfall, or Pereira would regard the Spaniards as being in a state of war against him.

Legazpi and the scribe, Hernan Riquel, were preparing a reply to this note at noon on the same day, when a message came that several of the small Portuguese craft were approaching. Shortly thereafter, the sound of cannonading arose. The Portuguese craft bombarded the works which were already on the bank at the watering-place. They then attacked the villages in the vicinity, killing numbers of the villagers. A few Spaniards were also killed in these actions.

Pereira's explanation afterwards was that the firing had been started by his orders merely in order to frighten off a number of soldiers and Filipinos who were at the watering-place, but that the Spanish artillery opened fire on his vessels. As for the Filipinos, they were, according to Pereira, dark people who had turned from their proper allegiance to Portugal and deserved what they got.

The next day Pereira sent two galiots and a pinnace to blockade the northern entrance to Port Zebu. His ships already had command of the southern entrance. By these means Pereira effectively prevented all ingress and egress both by the Spanish and Philippine craft, thereby stopping supplies of food from other islands from reaching the Spanish camp. Since Zebu was itself in poor shape for food, Pereira counted on this blockade to starve the Spaniards into submission.

Two months of stalemate followed, the Spaniards having the advantage of defence by virtue of their guns and fortifications, forcing the Portuguese ships to stay out of range, while the Portuguese had command of the sea. During this time great hardship prevailed in the Spanish camp, and the soldiers were reduced to hunting rats for food.

Eventually the same shortage of food which the Portuguese were enforcing on the Spaniards overtook the Portuguese themselves. On New Year's Day, 1569, Pereira raised the blockade and sailed off to the Moluccas. By way of farewell he sent a message saying that he would be back in due course with overwhelming forces, and would throw the Spaniards into the sea.

Meanwhile Felipe de Salcedo and the company of the *San Pablo*, while making for Mexico, had been having their adventures. They did not make sufficient northing after leaving the Philippines to get into the westerlies of high latitudes, and eventually fetched up at Guam in the Marianas.

Here the *San Pablo* dragged her moorings and went ashore.

The *San Pablo* had to be written off, being fast aground. They did however have the ship's boat. They decided to build it up into a small decked sailer which, with any luck, might get them back to the Philippines. They had materials for this in the wreck. It would be touch-and-go with 130 men on board, but was their only way out.

The artisans accordingly built decking and topsides onto the boat, and it was provisioned for the journey of some 1200 miles that lay ahead. When the season of the south-westerly monsoon was over, the entire ship's company squeezed into the little vessel, and entrusted themselves to Heaven and the sea. Both were kind, and they succeeded in getting back to the Philippines.

Some time after the Portuguese fleet had departed from Port Zebu, the Spaniards decided to move their main base to the island of Panay, to the north-west of the island of Zebu. Diego de Artieda, a veteran soldier who had come with Felipe de Salcedo from Mexico the previous year, inspected the proposed site and reported that it was in his opinion much superior from a military point of view to Port Zebu, where the Portuguese could bottle them up like rats in a trap without adequate food, as they had already proved. Panay, however, had a wide deep river, several miles from its mouth there was a site for a camp which could be strongly defended, and the hinterland was prolific in rice.

The heavy task of moving the camp, including the artillery, was accordingly undertaken, and the shift to Panay went on piecemeal for some time.

In July of 1569 the indefatigable Felipe de Salcedo set sail once more for Mexico, this time in the *San Lucas*.

When the *San Lucas* reached Mexico, Salcedo found his old friend Captain Juan de la Isla there. Isla told him that after leaving Zebu in 1567 in the *San Juan*, he had got to

Mexico and then sailed on round South America to Spain. There he had found Legazpi's eldest son Melchior de Legazpi, pleading his father's cause at the Spanish Court. Isla and others had been able to support Melchior's plea. The King had been pleased to confirm Legazpi in the title of Captain-General and Governor for life, with a salary of 2000 ducats per year from the revenues of Zebu. Furthermore an expedition with two hundred men and supplies was about to go to Legazpi's assistance.

The award of a salary of 2000 ducats from the revenues of Zebu was a trifle ironical, since there was little prospect of any revenues from Zebu for a long time.

Juan de la Isla reached Panay with an expedition in June 1570, leaving again for Mexico the following month. Later again Felipe de Salcedo in the *San Lucas* renewed his acquaintance with the Philippines. There are records of further trips by the *San Lucas* and the *San Juan* in the spectacular ferry service of 16,000 miles from Acapulco to the Philippines and back again which now developed. The *San Lucas* and the *San Juan* now sail out of our story, and with them Juan de la Isla and Felipe de Salcedo.

After the removal of the main camp to Panay, Captain Juan de Salcedo, Legazpi's grandson, made a trip to the north which was to have momentous results. The Spaniards had heard much of the northern islands of the Philippines from the traders who came from Luzon to Zebu. Mahomet, the first of these traders, had over the years become a close friend and follower of the Spaniards, making himself useful as an interpreter and intermediary with the local people. He brought his wife and son to Panay and all three became Christians.

Salcedo set off on his exploratory trip to the north with forty soldiers in several large native vessels, manned by Filipinos. They came up from Panay to Mindoro, the large

island north of Panay. On the west coast of Mindoro, they
had a tussle with one of the settlements, which they subdued
by force of arms. Then they moved on north to Lubang, an
island close to Luzon itself.

In Lubang Salcedo and his men saw evidence of the more
advanced ways of the northern islands. They found, for the
first time in the Philippines, forts defended with cannon.
When the Spaniards came to the first of these, the occupants
fired their culverins at them. There was a moat of water
round the fort, and the attackers were baffled for a time.
Then it was found that the defenders had carelessly left a
boat fastened to the fort in the moat, so two of the Spanish
soldiers swam to the boat under fire and brought the vessel
back with them. Fifteen soldiers then went in the boat with
their arquebuses and stormed the fort, capturing it. In it
they found twelve culverins. Salcedo and his men later came
to a second fort in Lubang, where the defenders held them
off all day. Eventually the fort capitulated, and the defenders
paid Salcedo a tribute of 100 taels of gold, which was divided
among the soldiers as booty of war.

When Juan de Salcedo got back to Panay, things there were
in poor shape. The Spaniards had thought that they would
have plenty of food there, and that the Portuguese would not
be able to starve them out. But a plague of locusts descended
on the Panay crops and continued to infest the island. The
resulting shortage of food obliged Legazpi to put numbers
of men on other islands, thereby weakening their military
strength in the face of the expected attack by the Portuguese.
The river at Panay furthermore proved unsuitable for big
ships. What they needed, as they had ever since they came
to the Philippines, was a good port with assured supplies of
food.

These factors caused them to be interested in Luzon itself.
Mahomet and his brother, who had joined him at Panay,
were natives of Manila in Luzon.

Goite and Salcedo were accordingly deputed by Legazpi to go to Luzon on an exploratory trip, taking Mahomet and his brother with them.

On 8 May, 1570, Goite and Salcedo left Panay with ninety soldiers and twenty sailors in a locally constructed small sailing ship, called the *San Miguel*, and a pinnace, together with fifteen large native canoes manned by Filipinos.

Coming up to Mindoro, Goite heard that two junks from China were at the island, so he and his flotilla set out in search of them. Some of Goite's men went ahead of the *San Miguel* in some of the smaller vessels. When Goite and Salcedo caught up with them, they found that the advance party had captured the Chinese junks and had inflicted much damage on them.

When Goite asked the leader of the advance party how this had happened, it was explained that when the advance vessels had come into the bay, the junks had borne down on them side by side, with drums beating and fifes playing, firing rockets and culverins. The junks were large and high, and the Spanish vessels were low, but despite this disadvantage the Spanish musketeers had won the day, and the junks had been boarded.

The ships proved to be trading craft with silk, gold thread, gilded porcelain vases, musk, cottons, earthenware, iron and copper.

Goite gave one of the junks back to the Chinese so that they could return to their own country, and sent the other with its samples of Chinese ware to Legazpi at Panay. Because the rig of the junk was entirely strange to the Spaniards, four Chinese sailors went along with the vessel.

Goite and Salcedo then heard that there was a very strong fortified port at another part of the Mindoro coast. They decided to go there and show the flag.

As they entered the port, they saw that it was a superb

defensive site. A very steep hill was fortified with a stone wall at its base fourteen feet thick. All along the hillside culverins were mounted. The defenders were ranged on the slope. They wore showy head-coverings, and there was much beating of drums, blowing of horns and ringing of bells in token of defiance.

The brave and impetuous Goite decided to go with Mahomet and only a couple of soldiers to parley with the defenders. When Goite and Mahomet reached the foot of the hill, Goite told Mahomet to tell the chiefs that he came to treat for their friendship. After some argument among themselves, the defenders sent down an envoy, who came scrambling down the steep slope almost on all fours. He recognized Mahomet, who was well known in the islands, and they embraced.

It was agreed that there should be peace, and Goite then put on a very fine review. His company of soldiers drilled in perfect order and fired their muskets, and the cannon on the *San Miguel* fired a salvo.

Even before this display was ended, one of the Mindoro chiefs came forward with sixty taels of gold and gave it to Goite, saying that they would deliver in due course a tribute of four hundred gold taels in all.

Friendly contacts then were developed between the people of the little settlement and the Spaniards. The village comprised tall huts, and the inhabitants showed so much gaiety that they resembled children at play.

From Mindoro Goite passed over with his little fleet to the south-west coast of Luzon. Here, Mahomet and his brother told them, they were not far from Manila Bay.

As they were going along the coast, Mahomet pointed out a narrow estuary, and explained that it led to a big lake with a volcano in it. There was a fortified town on the lake.

Through this estuary into the lake went Juan de Salcedo

with some of the small vessels, accompanied by Mahomet.
When they rejoined Goite, Salcedo had quite a story to tell.
When they got into the lake they approached the site of the
fort, passing through some narrow waters with high ground
on each side. Suddenly arrows were fired at them from the
heights, although they could not see anybody. Their
musketeers fired a volley in return. One of the arrows hit
Salcedo in the leg, and it was fortunate that there were
canvas guards on the boats, since otherwise there would
have been more casualties. Mahomet said that the arrow
which hit Salcedo would be poisoned, and got a herb to
bind on the wound as an antidote. When they got to the
town, the defenders shot arrows for a while, but the Spanish
muskets soon put them to flight. When the Spaniards went
into the town, they found several Chinese captives with their
faces flayed and exposed to the sun. Some of them were
already dead. Two of them who were still living were freed,
and explained that they were the survivors of a trading junk
which had come to the town. When they had wanted to leave
the local people had tried to prevent them, so the junks had
fired a culverin and killed a local chief. But the junks were
wrecked on the shoals in the estuary, and the crews were all
captured.

Soon after this, Goite and Salcedo and their fleet came
into Manila Bay. They saw the village of Manila on a point of
land between a river and the sea. Mahomet and his brother
advised them to seek anchorage a few miles along the bay
from Manila, and this they did.

Salcedo and Goite decided that this was the big port with
plenty of food which they had been looking for. The land
around the bay looked very inviting, with cultivations every-
where.

It was now arranged that Mahomet's brother should go to
Manila as Goite's envoy. After three days he came back with

one of the officers of Raja Soliman, the chief of Manila, who
sent a message that he would receive the Spaniards in peace
and let them settle there.

Goite's ships then came to the bar of the river at Manila.
They found an extensive settlement. The town was defended
by a palisade, with numbers of cannon protruding through
large openings.

Opposite the town, at the mouth of the river, Goite's
ships came to anchor. On the beach a considerable gathering
of the residents of Manila gazed curiously at the Europeans.

A little farther off in the river were four Chinese junks.
They sent over to the *San Miguel* some skiffs bearing gifts of
rice, hens and silk. It was the first instalment of a huge trade
in Manila Bay that went on between Spaniard and Chinese for
several centuries.

Raja Soliman's uncle now came forward to meet Goite,
and then Raja Soliman himself arrived. He gave himself
considerable airs, saying that if any offence were done to the
dignity of Manila, it would be repaid in kind. A friendly
arrangement was, however, agreed upon between him and
Goite.

Later on the Spaniards found that the Mohammedanism
of the 'Moros' of Luzon was rather superficial, like their
exotic names. Most of them ate pork, only those who had
visited Borneo taking the Moslem prohibition against this
seriously.

The next day Raja Soliman sent a message to Goite saying
that he had heard that the Spaniards intended to ask for
tribute, and that so far from paying this he would forbid
them from entering the river.

No sooner did Goite receive this message than, characteris-
tically, he went ashore to Soliman's house with only an
interpreter and one or two supporters, and asked to see the
chief.

When Soliman came into the reception room in his house, which was adorned with Chinese art and Philippine gold ornaments, Goite proceeded to reassure him, saying that no thought of asking tribute had arisen. All they asked, said Goite, was to be allowed to stay at Manila, and to buy food.

Raja Soliman, much mollified, agreed to this compact. He and Goite then went through the ceremony of drinking blood and wine.

Raja Soliman and the warriors of Manila, however, were not reconciled for long to the presence of the European visitors. Soon they were conspiring to attack them unawares. They proposed to do this when rain was falling, since the Spaniards would find it more difficult to set off their firearms.

These plots soon came to the ear of Goite through his Philippine friends. He accordingly arranged for a careful watch to be kept at all times by guards both on the ships and on shore.

In order to divert the attention of the Spaniards, part of the strategy of Soliman and his supporters was to represent to the visitors that the people of other parts of Manila Bay were planning to attack them.

Now as the days went by, the weather remained fine, without the rain that the strategists of Manila were waiting for. Things came to a head one day when a number of canoes were seen coming across the bay from another part. Some of the Spaniards went to investigate. The Manila generals decided this was a good time to make their assault.

The Manila guns, poking through the large openings in the palisade in front of the town, opened fire on the Spanish vessels. One ball went through the side of the *San Miguel* and lodged in the casting room. Two other balls passed just above the deck.

The Spanish soldiers on shore, being on the alert for trouble, immediately charged the palisade. The architects of the Manila fortifications had made the mistake of making the openings in the palisade for the guns quite large. The counter-attackers were able to squeeze through them and come to close quarters with the artillerymen inside. In a short time the artillery was seized and the defenders were in flight. The people of Manila, using that speed in evacuation which was part of the condition of survival in the ancient warfare of the Philippines, forsook the town and fled up the river. The Spaniards subjected the retreating canoes to the indignity of being bombarded with their own cannon.

The Spanish soldiers followed up this victory by dispersing through the town, looking for valuables. At this Goite became much alarmed, because of the possibility of a counter-attack by the people of Manila. Impetuously he ordered the town to be put to the torch. The flames roared through the flimsy native houses, and soon the town was burned out.

Goite and Salcedo, having declared possession of Manila in the name of the King of Spain, returned to Panay. When they reported what had happened, Legazpi was much upset over the burning of Manila, since he had hoped for the friendship of the Manila chiefs. He was, however, much attracted by the good reports of Manila itself.

After some months, during which fears of the Portuguese, and the shortage of food at Panay, continued to agitate Legazpi and his associates, it was decided to move the main Spanish centre to Manila. This time there was no opposition from Raja Soliman, who sought and was given pardon for his assault on Goite's ships. The historic occupation of Manila by Legazpi took place in May of 1571.

It was not written in the book of Fate that the Portuguese should dislodge the Spaniards from the Philippines. Chief Captain Pereira did not in fact reappear to embarrass them. In due course Legazpi and his captains consolidated their hold on Manila and the surrounding countryside.

On 20 August, 1572, Legazpi, having risen that morning in Manila in seemingly good health, suddenly went into a decline and died.

Fame, but not fortune, was Legazpi's reward for calling into being a new Spanish empire in the Philippines. His estate in Manila was insufficient to pay his debts there, his insolvency being partly due to his having used some of his money to help his soldiers. The Viceroy of New Spain had to intercede with the King to provide Legazpi's son Melchior with lands in Mexico for the support of Melchior's unmarried sisters.

Martin de Goite later met his death in Manila in spectacular circumstances. Juan de Salcedo and most of the Spanish troops were away from Manila on a campaign. Goite remained in Manila with a small garrison. A Chinese pirate called Lim On Hon chose this time to make an attack on Manila. He sailed into Manila Bay with a fleet of seventy vessels. In the ensuing fighting Goite was killed and Manila was captured. Juan de Salcedo and the Spanish troops, having seen Lim On Hon's fleet making for Manila, followed it along the coast. They attacked the pirates to such good effect that Lim On Hon withdrew with his vessels to another part of Luzon. Eventually the Spaniards drove Lim On Hon and his pirate horde out of the islands with the assistance of a squadron of Chinese junks under a legitimate Chinese admiral.

Juan de Salcedo, after a brief career of military glory in Luzon, died at the early age of 25 years.

Thus ends the story of the exciting adventures which befell the men of the *San Pedro*, the *San Pablo*, the *San Juan* and the *San Lucas* when they sailed to the Isles of the West four centuries ago. By the mortality of human flesh it was not in the nature of things that Legazpi and Andres de Urdaneta and Mateo del Saz and Martin de Goite and Felipe de Salcedo and Juan de la Isla and Alonso de Arellano should know what they started when they took the ships out of La Navidad on that fine day in November 1564. Even less of the sequel was known to Lope Martin and his fellow-conspirators marooned on Ujelang, or by the much-stabbed Pericon and his foolish son, or by Ortiz de Mosquera and Bartolomé de Lara who were hanged and drowned in their shackles, or by Pierres Plun and Jorge the Greek who lost their heads at Zebu. By looking in the glass of history we can see something of the vista that lay ahead.

Miguel Lopez de Legazpi was the first of a long succession of Spanish governors of the Philippines. By founding Manila and making contact with the Chinese junks there he opened up the way to the procession of treasure ships which sailed from Acapulco in Mexico to Manila and back. The Portuguese wilted away in Java and the Moluccas before the Dutch, and their place as would-be harassers of the Spanish ships was taken by Netherlanders who, in the first half of the 17th century, made it their sport to lie in wait for the silver-ships as they made for Manila. Later the English took a hand in this pastime, and Anson brought off his coup of forcing the treasure galleon of 1743 to strike its colours and yield up its cargo near Manila. These assaults were, however, but as pin-pricks in the steady flow of Mexican silver to Manila and thence to the treasuries of the East Indian and Chinese potentates. For three centuries after Legazpi, Spanish ships sailed to the Isles of the West, returning to Mexico laden with the gold, spices, silks and art of the gorgeous Orient.

A NOTE ON SOURCES

THE sources for this book, apart from those mentioned in the following two sentences of this note, are contained in that publication of the Spanish archives known as *Colección de Documentos Ineditos Relativos al Descubrimiento Conquista y Organizatión de las Antiguas Posesiones Españolas de Ultramar. Segunda Serie*. Vols. 2, 3. *De las Islas Filipinas*. Madrid, 1886-7. The sources relating to the clash between Legazpi's and Pereira's forces at Zebu (see Chapter 12), to Juan de Salcedo's and Martin de Goite's visits to the northern Philippines (see Chapter 12), and to the conquest of Manila (see Chapter 12) are contained in *The Philippine Islands*, Eds. E. H. Blair and J. A. Robertson. Vols. 2, 3. Cleveland, 1903-4. Some details of the reception of Arellano after the return of the *San Lucas* to Mexico (see Chapter 7), and of the attack of the Chinese pirate Lim On Hon on Manila (see Chapter 12), are contained in Antonio de Morga, *Sucesos de las Islas Philipinas*. Mexico, 1609.

Index

PRINTED BY WHITCOMBE AND TOMBS LIMITED—G4708